Pew & Pavement

PEW & PAVEMENT

STORIES FROM AN URBAN CHURCH

DAVID A. SHIREY

Front cover art by Towseef Dar, Adobe Stock #482843447

Book cover and interior design by Adam Thomas.

ISBN: 979-8-9883293-2-9 (paperback)
ISBN: 979-8-9883293-3-6 (e-book)

This book is memoir. It reflects the author's recollections of experiences
nearly four decades ago. Though all the incidents are real, the author, a
storyteller at heart, has told them in a way that evokes the feeling and
meaning of what took place. Embellishments? Yes. Fabrications? No.
The dialogue comes from the author's recollections and journals. It does
not represent word-for-word transcripts, though some is verbatim. It
does convey the character and personality of the speakers. All persons within are actual individuals; there are no composite or fictional
characters. No effort has been made whatsoever to disguise the author's
abiding appreciation and affection for the people whose stories are
chronicled in these pages.

Printed in the United States of America.

David A. Shirey
3085 Montavesta Rd.
Lexington, KY 40502

www.davidashirey.com

For all the saints of
Compton Heights Christian Church
(Disciples of Christ)

"Seek the welfare of the city where I have sent you …
and pray to the Lord on its behalf, for in its welfare
you will find your welfare."
(Jeremiah 29:7)

Contents

Introduction: No April Fools

"The members of Compton Heights always have been a resilient group, and problems were faced with faith and resoluteness."
–The Rev. Agnes Sierat-Taylor
A Brief History: Compton Heights Christian Church (Disciples of Christ) 1894-1994

"We have no people of large means in the church, but everybody helps a little, and that enables us to carry the load."
–The Rev. J. L. Parsons,
Compton Heights founding pastor, 1894

"This church is a thoroughly missionary church."
–Compton Heights Herald, 1925

"One of the milestones in the life of your church is about to be realized. The old mansion served for some twenty years, and we made do ... Our goal of an adequate building is about to be realized. The new building offers a challenge to our church program and to the way we serve, that they may reflect God's will and meet the needs of those in our community."
– The Rev. Dr. G. Hugh Wilson, 1963

"In 2001, Compton Heights Christian Church formally de-clared ourselves to be an Open and Affirming Congregation; yet that declaration is never where the journey begins. As I look at the history of CHCC, I am convinced that the journey began long, long ago."
  –The Rev. Dr. Jacque Foster, 2001

Compton Heights Christian Church (Disciples of Christ) was founded on April 1, 1894, on St. Louis' near south side at the corner of California and St. Vincent Avenues, one mile northeast of its current location on S. Grand Ave. and Flora Place. Over the 130 years of its existence, the congregation's salt of the earth people, faithful to Christ's example and calling, have worshipped God and served their urban neighbors from pew to pavement with resilience, generosity, and inclusiveness.

Agnes Sierat-Taylor was right. Compton is a resilient congregation. Two years after its founding, May 27, 1896, a deadly tornado cut a swath of devastation across the near south side of St. Louis. The storm killed 255 and injured 1,000 in just twenty minutes. It killed more people in less time than any disaster in St. Louis history and remains the third-deadliest tornado in United States history. More than 5,000 people were left homeless, including thirty families of the nascent Compton Heights Christian Church and 8,800 buildings were destroyed or significantly damaged, including Compton Heights' two-year-old chapel.

The Rev. J. L. Parsons, the church's founding pastor, wrote, "In the judgment of many, it is not worth repairing; our congregation is poor, and many of them have left." When he described his flock as people not of large means, "but everybody helps a little, and that enables us to carry the load," he could have been describing the Compton Heights of my era (1985-1989) and yet today. The hardy congregation persevered. With the assistance of local donors and other congregations, they rebuilt the chapel. In 1903, they built a new, larger building that served as their home for the next twenty-five years.

The growing congregation purchased a twenty-room mansion at S. Grand and Flora Place in 1925 with the intention of razing it and building a church only to be devastated once again, not by a twenty-minute cyclone, but a years-long legal battle over zoning/deed restrictions that went all the way to the Missouri Supreme Court. In 1929, while the case was being litigated, the congregation met in the Jewish Synagogue a few blocks west of their desired site. They remained there thirteen years, a foreshadowing of the spirit of ecumenicity and partnership that would blossom in the 1960s with the formation of a social service ministry called the Five Church Association (now Isaiah 58 Ministries) and Helping Hands Day Care Center (now Cornerstone Center for Early Learning).

The statement in the *Compton Heights Herald* in January 1925 that declared "This church is a thoroughly missionary church" was right. From its offerings nearly a century ago to help establish other new congregations in St. Louis (Clifton Heights/Watson Terrace Christian Church and Overland Park Christian Church) to its supporting home and overseas ministries of the Christian Church (Disciples of Christ) to its serving as a Living Link partner with missionaries in India and Japan to the welcoming and sponsoring of refugees and the ministries of the Five Church Association/Isaiah 58 Ministries and Helping Hands/Cornerstone Center, the congregation has embodied Swiss theologian Emil Brunner's dictum, "The Church exists by mission, just as a fire exists by burning."

Throughout the 1940s, the congregation met in the cramped quarters of the refurbished mansion until, legal obstructions finally resolved, the present sanctuary was dedicated in 1951 and the education building in 1963. Hugh Wilson was right when he acknowledged the long-awaited milestone of the new buildings and challenged the congregation to use them to "reflect God's will and meet the needs of those in our community." Compton's buildings and property at 2149 S. Grand have been beacons of hope, help, and hospitality from the day they were dedicated nearly seventy-five years ago to today.

Jacque Foster was right in 2001 when, after Compton Heights became an Open and Affirming congregation welcoming into its full life and ministry persons of all sexual orientations, gender identities, and gender expressions, she recognized the inclusiveness of God's love in Christ evidenced in that decision was but the latest fruit of the congregation's inclusive spirit, "a journey that began long, long ago." Compton Heights welcomed women to serve on the board of directors in 1919. In the 1920s, when a theological kerfuffle over "open membership" embroiled the Christian Church – the policy of accepting into church membership Christians who had not been baptized by immersion – Compton Heights took a stand welcoming one and all, regardless of how much water was used or when it was administered. The church was also on the vanguard of calling women to serve in leadership positions, including elder and pastor.

The founding of Compton Heights Christian Church on April 1, 1894, was no April Fools. God knew what God was doing. Truth be told, I sure didn't when I was called to serve them. But they did. They knew how to do ministry in their urban setting, and they were patient, gracious, and steadfastly supportive of their twenty-five-year-old pastor.

The Apostle Paul's description of the Christians in Corinth fits the congregation I was privileged to pastor: "Consider your own call, brothers and sisters: not many of you were wise by human standards, not many were powerful, not many were of noble birth" (1 Corinthians 1:26). God chose those Corinthians to carry out the risen Christ's work in their neighborhood just as God chose Fred and Lil, Cliff and Edna, Walt and Audrey, Lew and Carol, Millie, Jim and Sharon, Bob and Gladys, Neva, Tiny, and Bill, Wanda and Clarence, Paul, Sue and family, Pauline, Mary, Ella, Hazel, Lillian, Darrell and Marty, Kathy, Madeline, Marsha, Chris, Bonnie and Becky – all the people whose stories follow in these pages.

The wonder of wonders is they chose me to be their pastor for a formative period of my life – my first full-time pastorate.

I could not have been called to a better place and people.

I am indebted to them to this day.

Here are their stories.

Somewhere East of the Mississippi

Somewhere east of the Mississippi. That's the order I placed with God as I began the search for full-time employment.

I graduated from Vanderbilt Divinity School in May 1985. For nearly three years, I served the Carthage (TN) Christian Church (Disciples of Christ) in Smith County, an hour east of Nashville. Those two dozen people were my first love in ministry. They sat through my first attempts at preaching. They took turns having me over for Sunday dinner – fried chicken, collard greens, mashed potatoes, corn bread, and apple pie. When Miss Ella died, I did my first funeral. When Leann and Randy got married, I did my first wedding. When Jennie and I married in 1984, they hosted a shower for her and Lib, Leann's mother, made Jennie's wedding dress. At the ripe old age of twenty-two, they called me to be their pastor and on May 14, 1985, at age twenty-five, I knelt at the chancel steps and faced the communion table as they laid hands on me and ordained me.

The first hands laid upon me that day were Mr. Bill's. Alexander Campbell Read, Jr., affectionately called Mr. Bill, was the octogenarian head elder of the congregation. He single handedly called me to be the pastor of the church three years earlier. I substituted one Sunday for Pinckney Victor Love, Jr., who was graduating. Brother Love (I kid you not) had served as pastor for three years, the latest in a series of pastorates by Vanderbilt students dating to the 1950s, the last time the congregation could afford a full-time pastor.

The Wednesday following my subbing for Brother Love, there was a knock on the door of my apartment at the Disciples Divinity House. I had a call on the house phone downstairs. It was Mr. Bill.

"David Shirey," he said, "we had a congregational meeting after you left last Sunday. We've called you to be our pastor."

"But Mr. Read," I said, "I wasn't looking to be your pastor. I was just filling in."

"David Shirey," he responded, "That wasn't a question. That was a statement, son."

Hence my call to Carthage.

A couple months before my ordination, Mr. Bill asked if I would consider remaining their pastor after graduation. They would raise my weekly salary from $75 to $100 per week. Plus, if Jennie and I moved to Carthage from Nashville, we could live in the parsonage, a small house a few doors from the church that had been rented for the three decades they had been without a full-time pastor.

"We sure hate to see you and Jennie go," he said. "What do you think?"

I politely declined. Mr. Bill said he understood and then gifted us a wooden rocking chair from the parsonage.

"Take it with you as a memory of us," he said.

It's still with us forty years later.

I didn't tell Mr. Bill, but for several months I had been in Search and Call (our denomination's name for the process by which congregations looking for pastors and pastors looking for congregations can connect). When I filled in the section asking where we wanted to serve, I typed east of the Mississippi. I also noted we wanted to serve a church doing urban ministry.

We made the geographical request because I am from Ohio and Jennie is from Virginia. Our extended families lived closer to the Atlantic than the Mississippi, but we were willing to go as far west as Illinois, on whose eastern border my parents had moved when I was in high school. The request to go where we could do urban ministry was rooted in the clarion call to do justice we'd received at Vanderbilt via Micah's megaphone: "Do justice, love mercy, walk humbly" (Micah 6:4). Bottom line: we were open to God's call as long as it was between eastern Illinois and central Virginia.

We should have known we might not get our wish when in the fall of 1984 I got a telephone call from a search committee in rural Iowa. Not east of the Mississippi. Not urban ministry.

"Reverend Shirey," said the chair of the search committee, "We're calling from (I forget) Christian Church in (I forget), Iowa. How are you this evening?"

A half dozen "Midwest nice" folks then introduced themselves and told me of their love for their church with such sincerity that I did not dismiss the location and type of ministry out of hand.

They asked, "Would you be willing to farm?"

That's not a question I anticipated.

"Why do you ask?"

Their church owned several hundred acres of land they farmed together in addition to working their own farms. The money they received from the cooperative venture supplemented their operating budget and increased their outreach giving. They were looking for a pastor willing to farm alongside them.

I was intrigued. What came out of this city boy's mouth was, "I'd be willing to learn." What did not come out of my mouth was anything about Jennie's and my stated preference for urban ministry east of the Mississippi.

"Tell me more about your church," I said.

They did. When we said our goodbyes, they thanked me and said they'd get back with me. Days led to weeks and weeks to months. Six months later, it was spring of 1985. I was soon to be ordained, and I had heard nothing from Iowa.

I had heard, however, from a church in St. Louis. Urban ministry: check. East of the Mississippi: nope. Not quite. It dawned on me that perhaps God was stretching me. When it was time for me to choose a divinity school four years earlier, I ruled out Midwestern seminaries, sensing I needed to get out of my comfort zone. Nashville fit the bill. Vanderbilt's rigorous academic curriculum stretched me. I got a C on my first theology paper and was happy to receive a passing grade. Accepting the call to serve as pastor in Carthage stretched me as did translating the theological concepts and vocabulary I was learning at Vanderbilt into language that made sense to their ears. All that stretching was for the good. I suspected God was up to it again.

You said east of the Mississippi? I'm calling you four miles west of it. S-t-r-e-t-c-h.

The Danish theologian and philosopher Søren Kierkegaard said, "We live life forward, but understand it backward." Retrospectively, the willingness to be stretched first to Vanderbilt and Carthage and then west of the Mississippi to St. Louis introduced me to what has become a spiritual rule of thumb: growth happens when we step out in faith beyond the familiar. Safely cocooned in our comfort zones, we're in control (we think), but in circumstances when we're stretched, we must learn to become more reliant on God's guiding and more trusting in God's provision. A physical therapist told me, "If you're not challenged, you're not changing." Likewise with spiritual muscle. Being stretched is good for the soul.

It's not a life lesson Jennie and I readily grasped. When we were approached to start a new church seventeen years later, we put *east coast* as our geographical preference. We got Phoenix.

So it was that the day Mr. Bill made his goodhearted gesture of a $25 raise and a parsonage on Main Street in Carthage, I was in conversation with the search committee of Compton Heights Christian Church (Disciples of Christ) in St. Louis, MO. When they told me about their church, they did so with the same sincerity as the folks in Iowa. And, like the folks in Iowa, they asked if Jennie and I were willing to roll up our sleeves and join them in their place of ministry.

"David, we take our urban location as a calling from God to serve our neighbors. All of them. Every day. Would you and Jennie consider coming and joining us?"

I said I'd welcome a chance to visit. They said they'd fly me in and sent me a ticket.

As I was packing for the flight to St. Louis, the phone

rang. It was the church in Iowa apologizing for taking six months to get back with me. They wanted to fly me up to visit the church and the farm. I politely declined due to my being in conversation with another congregation and thanked them for their interest. They understood and wished me well in ministry.

What I understood was I had traded soybeans and corn for concrete and asphalt, either one a stretch.

What the Stonemason Said

I deboarded the plane and stood patiently. This was in pre-TSA screening days when arriving passengers were greeted at the gate by those waiting for them. The crowd thinned until I was among the only people left. Across the empty boarding area, I spotted a kindly-looking elderly man sporting a well-worn driver's cap and windbreaker, arms folded across his chest, smiling. Our eyes having met, he raised his hand in greeting. We walked toward each other.

"David Shirey?" he asked. "I'm Fred Kaley. Welcome to St. Louis. Let's go get your suitcase. I'm your cabbie for the day."

Years ago, I was cautioned, "Beware of who meets you at the station." The first to meet and greet the new boss are often people who have an agenda. Not Fred. He embodied humility, from the word humus – earth, as in "down to earth." As in Jesus' compliment of Nathanael, "Behold an Israelite in whom there is no guile" (John 1:47). As in "What you see is what you get, and what you get is downright good," which is what I said about Fred when I led his funeral three years later. Compton Heights sent a good man to meet me at the station.

His driving cap perched winsomely on his head, my cabbie asked, "Since we've got time before you meet with the search committee, how 'bout if I give you a tour of St. Louis?"

"Absolutely," I said.

Therewith commenced my guided tour of recent improvements to downtown St. Louis' streets, levees, and sewage/drainage system. Fred, a World War II vet and retiree from the Public Works Department, took great pride in showing me potholes repaired, levees fortified, streets repaved, and sewers redesigned for optimal drainage. Though the St. Louis Arch rose in splendor a few hundred yards away from the riverfront, Fred directed my gaze to a crew of hardhats laboring on a retaining wall along the Mississippi.

"I used to do that," he said in a tone of quiet satisfaction.

A story is told about a shoemaker who became a Christian. When he asked Martin Luther what work he should do as a follower of Jesus, Luther is quoted as saying, "Make a good shoe and sell it at a fair price." Some people think if we asked Jesus what he wants us to do with our lives he'd tell us to quit our day job, take vows of poverty and chastity, and live in a monastery. Fred lived out his calling by stewarding a city's infrastructure. He thereby blessed the lives of a million people of all races, ethnicities, and income levels, the majority of whom were ignorant of his labor and took what he did for granted. That didn't matter to Fred. His reward was serving the public with an honest day's labor done well. Call it vocation consecration.

When all is said and done, we're invited not just to make an offering on Sunday, but to be one all week. Paul wrote, "Take your everyday, ordinary life – your sleeping, eating, going-to-work, and walking-around life – and place it before God as an offering." (Romans 12:1, *The Message*). "Whatever you do, work at it with all your heart, as though you were working for the Lord and not for people" (Colossians 3:23, TEV). Fred lived out those verses on the concrete and asphalt streets of St. Louis and in the belly of its sewer system, not for praise or profit, but as an offering to God.

At Compton Heights, Fred was a deacon, a word that means servant. The same kindly face that greeted me at the airport graced us on Sundays. The calloused hands that wielded rake and shovel on the city's pavement passed bread and cup through the church's pews.

Years ago, I toured the National Cathedral in Washington, D. C. The tour guide learned I was a pastor and pointed to the top of the cathedral.

"Do you see the gargoyles at the top?" he asked.

"Barely," I said. "With binoculars I could see them better."

"That's my point," he said. "A story is told about the stonemason who worked on those gargoyles. That's all he did – chisel gargoyles out of stone. Someone noticed he was going into such elaborate detail and asked, 'Why are you spending so much time and effort on those things? They're so high up they won't even be seen by the people down below.' To which the stonemason responded, 'I'm not doing this for the people down below.'"

The stonemason's name was probably Fred.

Fred the Cabbie Redux

Fred Kaley served as my cabbie on my first visit to St. Louis, but when I arrived in August 1985 as Compton Heights Christian Church's called pastor, I met another member of the congregation named Fred who was a cabbie. The real thing. He worked as a dispatcher and driver for Yellow Cab Company. He also played the violin and sang in the choir. Which goes to show you there's no telling the talents people have. Who would guess the cab dispatcher/driver is also a classically trained violinist with perfect pitch?

I do not have perfect pitch. The previous sentence is a laugh line for my family. Four of five Shireys have musical aptitude. I do not. Which is where Fred the perfect pitch cabbie comes into the picture.

Lynwood Smith, Compton Heights' choir director who resembled Walt Disney, thought it would be a good idea if I sang as part of my installation service. He told me the choir would sing the hymn "The Voice of God is Calling" and in response I would sing the hymn "Lord, Speak to Me, That I May Speak" – call and response. Nice idea, except for the fact that I couldn't pick up the tune for the life of me. In rehearsals, the choir would call in perfect harmony and I would respond by a) failing to come in on the right beat, b) coming in off-pitch, or c) both of the above. Usually it was c). As the date of the installation service approached, I was nervous.

Fred the cabbie came to the rescue. He sat to the left of me at rehearsals in the bass section of the choir. When we sang and his perfect-pitch right ear heard my woefully imperfect-pitched squall, he extended his right hand and adjusted my pitch. If I was low, he'd turn his palm up and begin to raise his hand slowly, my voice modulating upward with his rising hand until I was at the right pitch. If I was too high, he'd turn his hand palm down and lower it until I was on pitch. Soon enough, I was reading the music (that's being generous) and, watching Fred's hand with my peripheral vision, raising or lowering my voice in concert with his hand. Imagine adjusting the tuner knob on a radio to reduce the static and lock into as clear a signal as possible. Such was the effect Fred's levitating hand had on my vocal cords.

When we stood on the chancel steps the day of my installation and sang, Fred stood to my left with his trusty right hand at the ready, hidden from view behind the sopranos in front of us. I may have come in too low or too high, I don't recall, but Fred quickly got me tuned in. My solo went fine.

Nearly forty years later, I was asked to introduce a church camp song as part of the children's message. I arrived early enough to go to the sanctuary and tell our accompanist what I was going to do.

"No problem," Kristi said, "I'll accompany you. Where are you starting?"

"At the beginning."

"No, I mean what pitch are you starting on?'"

"I haven't a clue."

She then played a note I tried to match. Unsuccessfully. She played it again. I needed Fred.

Another member of our congregation needed Fred, too. Pauline sat in the fourth pew, lectern side, window aisle. She was a literalist when it came to hymn singing. Psalm 100:1 says, "Make a joyful noise unto the Lord." A bumper sticker reads "God said it. I believe it. That settles it." Pauline made a joyful *noise* to the Lord with her voice. She loved the Lord, loved the old hymns, and loved to sing. So, she sang out – out loud and out of tune – and we loved her for the gusto with which she lifted her voice in praise to God.

In my four decades of serving churches, I've heard the gamut in music. Traditional. Contemporary. Blended. Voices with perfect pitch and others not so much. There's an age-old tension between inviting participation on the one hand and striving for excellence on the other. Invite everybody to sing and you get Pauline and me making our joyful noises. So much for excellence. Aspire for excellence and you'll get stirring music from gifted instrumentalists and pitch perfect vocalists whose singing will lift everyone's spirits, but to the exclusion of voices that need Fred.

Sometimes, I need to be quiet and let my spirit soar on the wings of others' songs. Other times, I want to stand next to Pauline and singers of our ilk and cut loose. Most every time, I find myself scanning my peripheral vision for the helpful hand that was graciously forbearing of my awkward attempts to respond to a congregation's call to be their pastor, patiently calling me forth to a higher plane … and pitch.

Look for a Steeple

Ronda's eyes were focused on a higher plane the day she exited I-44 and headed south on Grand Avenue. From my office window, I spotted a Ford Pinto pull over to a stop in front of the church. A young woman got out, walked in front of the car to the curb, and stepped up to the sidewalk. With her right hand shielding her eyes from the midday sun, she looked up at the steeple. I stepped outside to greet her.

After introductions, I asked, "How long have you lived in St. Louis?"

She looked at her watch and said, "About three hours."

I glanced at the Pinto, filled with her earthly belongings. She explained she was an Army brat and had moved "probably twenty times" while growing up. She remembered her parents telling her the first thing they did when they moved to a new city: "We looked for a steeple." Ours was the first steeple south of I-44.

Compton's steeple wasn't anything out-of-the-ordinary. Its white spire was proportional to the building beneath, a balance that would have received the approval of Jennie's father. Dick Taylor served in the Pacific Theater in World War

II. Educated to be an architect, at war's end he felt a call to ministry that he exercised with the utmost integrity, passion, and grace for the next 40+ years. One of the Rev. Dr. Richard F. Taylor's pet peeves was steeples that were out of proportion to the sanctuaries upon which they sat or too ostentatious for the manger-born carpenter of Nazareth whose church they marked. Compton's modest white cross atop its modest brick sanctuary would have passed Dick's architectural and theological inspection.

Having inspected the steeple from her Pinto and trusting it to be the welcome beacon for which her parents counseled her to look, Ronda asked what time worship would be on Sunday. She was warmly welcomed and sat in a pew near Fred and Lil. I don't know if Fred offered her a tour of recent improvements done under the auspices of the St. Louis Public Works Department, but I do know Lil took a liking to Ronda and invited her to sit with them.

From that day on, Ronda was under the shelter of Compton's steeple and people. When she showed up with a man she was dating, we welcomed Denny. When they announced their engagement, you'd have thought Fred and Lil's only granddaughter was getting married, so delighted were they for Ronda. The wedding was at Compton. When the couple announced they were expecting a child, Lil, Mary, Ella, Hazel, Edna, and company scheduled a baby shower in Fellowship Hall, and when Lisa was born, I dedicated her amid a sanctuary full of adopted grandparents, aunts and uncles. Looking for and finding a steeple, Ronda found a church family among whom she began her own family.

Two millennia earlier, an unmarried young woman pregnant with child left her home in small-town Nazareth of Galilee. Guided by the same homing device as Ronda, she headed toward a steeple of safety and welcome – her kinswoman Elizabeth's house. If one of Mary's reasons for making haste to leave Nazareth was the cloud of suspicion and judgment her pregnancy evoked, her reason for making haste to Elizabeth's house was her belief that a welcoming mercy awaited her. In Robert Frost's words, "Home is the place where when you have to go there, they have to take you in." Her world turned upside down, Mary made haste to the one place she knew she would be safe: Elizabeth's House.

Would that every church be an Elizabeth's House Christian Church – a place of refuge and shelter in a world quick to shame and judge, a place where runaways from whatever circumstances know they can find a house filled with grace-filled Aunt Elizabeths and Uncle Zechariahs, Lils and Freds, who will welcome them.

One day, a passerby paused in front of the church and stood transfixed in front of the sanctuary. I walked out to greet her. She said she was impressed by what she called "the big thing on top of the building."

"That's called a steeple," I said.

"Well," she said, "it looks real nice up there. Is it useable?"

I had never given any thought to the "useability" of "the big thing on top of the building." Was she wondering if there were big brass bells up there that tolled on the hour? Perhaps a carillon that would serenade the Shaw Neighborhood with hymns? Maybe she thought the big thing was the antenna for Radio Compton, outlet for my budding televangelist career.

I do know people pass by buildings with big things on

top and identify those buildings as churches. And I know that many wonder not about the useability of steeples but the useability of the people who populate the buildings beneath them. Are Christians good for anything? Oliver Wendell Holmes, Sr., father of the Supreme Court justice, said, "Some people are so heavenly minded that they are no earthly good." Is the Christian faith useable, capable of transforming lives and changing this world for the good? It is if it welcomes runaways like Mary and wayfarers like Ronda and celebrates their children – Mary's boy, Ronda's girl, and everybody else's sons and daughters.

Two years after Ronda pulled up in front of our church, she stopped to say she and her family had been transferred. "I want to say goodbye," she said, "and ask you if there is a Christian Church in Rockville, Maryland."

I found a congregation in my directory and gave her the address. As I walked back to my office, I shielded my eyes and looked up at the big thing on top of the building, glad for all it represents at its best, glad it caught the eye of Ronda and brought her to us.

As she got into her Pinto, car seat visible in the back, I cupped my hand to my mouth and shouted, "Look for a steeple, Ronda!"

A Barber's Prayers

Cliff knew that steeple up close and personal. A retired barber whose shop was attached to the side of his and Edna's modest home, Cliff was an elder, tenor in the choir, evangelism committee member, man of prayer, handyman par excellence, steel pedal guitarist, and steadfast encourager of his young pastor.

I am a fortunate man. Many people have blessed my life through the years. The visage of a precious few shimmer in my remembrance regularly. Cliff is one.

I was in the office one day, looking out toward where Ronda had pulled up in her packed Pinto, when the phone rang. It was Cliff's wife Edna.

"David, would you go check on Clifford?"

"Where is he?"

"I think he's up on the roof checking on a leak."

"Another one?"

"Apparently it's dripping down into the food pantry."

I climbed up to the roof. Cliff was sitting with his back against the base of steeple, his Bible open and his toolbox at this side. He looked up as I walked over.

"Cliff, Edna called. She was wondering when you might be back."

He looked at his watch, smiled, and said sheepishly, "I guess I lost track of time."

"How's the roof?"

"Oh, it's fine. I ran a bead of caulk along the base of the steeple here where I think some water might have been seeping in. We'll see."

Looking into the distance, he extended his arm and his hand swept across the two-story brick flats that lined the densely populated streets of the Shaw Neighborhood. "You can see the whole neighborhood and all the way downtown from here. Sometimes I just sit here, look out in every direction, and pray."

"May I join you?"

"Of course."

I sat down next to him, my back against the steeple. Edna would need to wait for a return call and a returned husband.

I can see him in my mind's eye: that silver-haired man with the expansive spirit filled with Christ-love. He has a toolbox and an open Bible, veteran of who-knows-how-many Stewardship Campaigns on a barber's salary, and he's praying for thousands of people north, south, east, and west from his perch at the base of a steeple.

One year before I got there, Cliff installed three speakers in the steeple. A crackerjack carpenter/engineer/do-it-yourselfer, he rigged up an unnecessarily complicated, yet effective system whereby Christmas music could be played through the speakers, sending Season's Greetings wafting through the neighborhood for all to hear … whether they wanted to or not.

Cliff sang in the tenor section of the choir alongside 80+ year-old Don Morrow, an equally sweet soul, who with his wife Alma made a ten mile commute over the Mississippi and past the Arch to Compton Heights from their house in East St. Louis, IL, one of the few white residents in the impoverished, predominately African American city. Cliff's son Darrell sat next to Don and Cliff in the choir, then Fred the cabbie, his levitating hand tuning my pitch, then me and bass Jim Clayton. The sight of Cliff singing in profile was a silhouette of piety at its most sincere – a soul "lost in wonder, love, and praise."

But lest you think Cliff's steeple supplications were but a "sweet hour of prayer" spent in intercession for the care of souls from the safe distance of a rooftop, know that his desire for our neighbors to know the abundant and eternal life that is the fruit of life in Christ was coupled with a longing for equity and equality for all God's children. Evangelism and social justice are two sides of the same gospel coin. "Seek the welfare of the city where I have sent you into exile," said Jeremiah, "and pray to the Lord on its behalf, for in its welfare you will find your welfare" (Jeremiah 29:7). Prophet and barber both yearned and prayed for the welfare of the city.

Fifteen years before I arrived, Cliff and the Compton Heights congregation joined with two Presbyterian churches (PCUSA), a United Church of Christ, and a United Methodist congregation to found an ecumenical social service ministry known as Five Church Association (FCA). 50+ years later, it is now called Isaiah 58 Ministries.

Isaiah's call to justice:
Is not this the kind of fasting I have chosen:
to loose the chains of injustice
*   and untie the cords of the yoke,*
to set the oppressed free and break every yoke?
Is it not to share your food with the hungry
*   and to provide the poor wanderer with shelter—*
when you see the naked, to clothe them,
*   and not to turn away from your own flesh and blood?*
Then your light will break forth like the dawn,
*   and your healing will quickly appear;*
then your righteousness will go before you,
*   and the glory of the Lord will be your rear guard.*
(Isaiah 58:6-8)

Isaiah 58 Ministries' Mission Statement:
Claiming our unity in Christ, in partnership with other churches, in celebration of the human community, and in common service with other faiths and secular organizations, we intend to:

- Provide programs and services to meet the physical and spiritual needs of persons in our neighborhood and in our churches.
- Promote opportunities for an ecumenical witness to Christ in the inner city and to exist as a sign of unity in a fragmented church and society.
- Work cooperatively with other church and community groups for the building up of the human community and alleviation of human problems such as hunger, poverty, racism, and injustice.

Four of the original five churches of Five Church Association/Isaiah 58 Ministries are no more. The Shaw Avenue United Methodist Church departed Five Church Association before my arrival, closed in 2004, reopened as The Word at Shaw in 2011, then closed again a few years ago. For several years, First Divine Science Church took its place. Tyler Place Presbyterian Church (PCUSA) dissolved a decade ago. Its building now houses a congregation of the Presbyterian Church in America (PCA). Years earlier, Peters Memorial Presbyterian Church (PCUSA) closed, its building now home to a Southern Baptist congregation. The last time I drove by what was St. Luke's United Church of Christ, the sign out front that used to list the times for worship and Sunday school touted the home of Stray Dog Theater (Mission statement: "Unleashing the art of theater, education, and community"). The art being unleashed on the stage which had been St. Luke's chancel included *Vampire Lesbians of Sodom*, *Godspell*, and *Saturday Night Fever*. As humorist Dave Barry used to write, "You can't make this stuff up!"

Compton Heights is the sole remaining founding congregation of Isaiah 58 Ministries, still steadfastly supporting it through financial offerings, volunteers, and the provision of space for its offices and outreach services. There is no telling how many tens of thousands of men, women, youth, and children have been fed, clothed, and provided utility assistance, counseling, job referrals, pastoral care, spiritual nourishment, and prayer over the past half-century thanks to Isaiah 58's ecumenical ministry.

Five Church Association's newsletter during my tenure at Compton Heights was called *Pew & Pavement*, a succinct summation of the partner churches' desire to live out the Great Commandment's call to love God and love neighbor in their urban setting.

In another nod to Kierkegaard's dictum that "We live life forward, but understand it backward," Jennie's and my expressed desire to do urban ministry somewhere east of the Mississippi was answered by our being stretched westward to Compton Heights and Five Church Association's pew and pavement ministry on St. Louis' near Southside, a ministry of grit and grace birthed in part and sustained in incalculable ways by a prophet's mandate and a barber's prayers.

First Among Equals

The Rev. Mildred "Millie" Slack was the answer to the barber's prayers and many others when the Five Church Association was born in 1970. A native of Hermann, MO, and a graduate of Lexington Theological Seminary, Millie was Executive Director when I arrived in 1985 and remained in that position of servant leadership until she retired in 2007 after thirty-seven years. The Rev. Brenda Booth has served as Executive Director since Millie's retirement; fifty-four years of selfless service by two tirelessly faithful women.

On my "Come and see" visit to Compton in the spring of 1985 when I was picked up by Fred and given the St. Louis Public Works tour, he delivered me to Millie's office on the second floor of the church's education building. The search committee was making a not-so-subtle statement: "If you come here to be our pastor, you will serve alongside Millie as mentor and colleague in a shared ministry from pew to pavement. You said you wanted to do urban ministry? Open wide and say 'ah.' There's a heaping helping to be done. Ask Millie. Learn from Millie. Follow Millie's lead and example."

For the four years I served as Compton's pastor, Millie

was my colleague and my pastor. The concrete and asphalt of St. Louis' streets are challenging soil for gospel seed, but the fruit of the Spirit took root in Millie: "Love, joy, peace, patience, kindness, gentleness, faithfulness, self-control" (Galatians 5:22). The whole package. She is among the saints of God.

Dr. Cornel West said, "Never forget that justice is what love looks like in public." I've been blessed in all my churches to have been in the company of men and women who didn't as much teach me as lived for me what that means. Millie was the first.

Next came Dr. Joseph Windley, who took me under his wing during the decade of my thirties when I served my second church. A respected senior statesman among African American pastors in Wilmington, NC, he was a veteran of the civil rights movement and pastor of our church's longtime custodian, Rosa McZek. When I arrived in Wilmington, Rosa wanted me to meet her pastor. Dr. Windley befriended me and invited me to tag along with him to meetings of the Black Clergy Caucus in Wilmington. I may have been the only white face there. In Dr. Windley's company, I was a welcome and honored guest.

In my early forties, the late J. Irwin Miller, CEO of Cummins Engine Company in Columbus, IN, a man of great intellect, faith, and decency, regularly invited me for lunch at his office, during which he asked my opinion on issues of justice and the common good.

Early in my ministry there, Joan, our secretary, buzzed my office phone.

"David, Mr. Miller is on the phone. He'd like to know if

you have a moment to talk."

"Of course. Put him through."

The annual stockholders meeting was in the offing, Mr. Miller was meeting with the Cummins board, and they were discussing the implications of EPA fuel economy guidelines on the design of their diesel engines. Mr. Miller wanted not only to meet, but exceed EPA guidelines, a decision that would require costly updates to production costs and cut into the bottom line, a path some of the board members cautioned would not be well received by shareholders. However, Mr. Miller's business sense was imbued with a desire to do God's business, in this case, exercising stewardship over God's creation by reducing the consumption of fossil fuels. The board was taking a break before coming back to decide and he wanted his pastor's opinion before proceeding. I have rarely felt as out of my league or as respected. I have no recollection of what I told him or whether it was of any worth.

One Lent during my Compton years, I taught a video-based class called *Questions of Faith*. One of the questions was, "What gives life meaning?" The presenter was Dr. Peggy Way, one of my professors at Vanderbilt. One thing that gives life meaning, Peggy counseled, is knowing who you are not. Know your gifts and your limitations. Do what you are gifted to do and, in the areas where you are not gifted, be a supportive presence to those who are.

In my journal, I noted Jennie had asked me, "Do you think we're all called to be social activists?" As I pondered her query in light of Peggy's wisdom, I wrote an entry:

Perhaps I have learned a bit about who I am not. Not a community organizer, social worker, or prophetic figure. There are these folks, thank God, in the Body of Christ. I can support them. I, perhaps, am a pastor, preacher, teacher, and follower/supporter of those who forge the way through the wilderness of sin/injustice striving to show/find the path of righteousness.

John Wesley said, "The world is my parish." I've been blessed to pastor churches that didn't just allow but expected me to be active in the communities I have served, with pulpit, pen, and life applying scripture and theology to the public sphere and acting on that intersection.

In each of my churches, I had a Millie, a Joseph, an Irwin, men and women who showed me what it looks like to "do justice and love mercy" while yet "walking humbly with God." Millie was first among equals.

Gold Stamp Guarantee

Contrast Compton Heights' and Millie's dedication to nitty gritty ministries of love and justice to real world neighbors with so-called ministries that have an eerily *other*worldly focus.

In May, 2011, the church Jennie and I planted in Arizona held our first worship service in our new building. We met in an elementary school cafeteria for eight years prior. In the days leading to the dedicatory service, I was asked if I knew the world was going to end six days after our first worship service, a prophecy made with tongue firmly in cheek.

I feigned shock and disbelief. "What? You mean to tell me we've worked our tails off for eight years only to have the world come to an end the week after our first worship service? Why didn't God tell me this sooner?"

Harold Camping, a televangelist who raked in more money in a year than the Five Church Association did in fifty years, prophesied the end of the world. It would commence on May 11, 2011, whereupon the saved would be taken up to heaven in the rapture, and, according to a *Washington Post* article, "there would follow five months of fire, brimstone, and plagues on Earth, with millions of people dying each day, culminating on October 21, 2011, with the final destruction of the world."

Camping broadcast his Doomsday prophesy via his media empire, social media, and a billboard at Camelback Rd. and 7th Ave. in bustling uptown Phoenix. I drove past the billboard on the eve of the end of the world and our first worship service with Sue, one of our members, to pick up janitorial supplies for the new building. I don't remember the exact wording. All I remember was a gold stamp embossed on it and the words GUARANTEED BY THE BIBLE.

Spoiler alert: Camping's prophesy did not come to pass. What did come to pass was our inaugural worship service in the new sanctuary that was not broadcast on the airwaves or plastered on a downtown billboard, followed by years of service to God and neighbor not reported by the *Washington Post*. Likewise, back in St. Louis, the ministries of Compton Heights and the Five Church Association continued without fanfare.

Authoritative pronouncements made by self-proclaimed prophets who bank (literally) on gullible folks' willingness to believe God has made some people privy to insider trading secrets about the end times to which the rest of us rank-and-file Christians have no access irks me. The way I look at it, there are innumerable things a disciple of Jesus can do that are of more consequence to the kingdom of God than conjuring an end-of-the world countdown clock from bogus interpretations of Scripture. If you're going to obsess over figuring something out, figure out the whys and wherefores behind poverty, racism, and Alzheimers. If you must crunch numbers, balance the federal budget.

The worst thing about the Doomsday prophesying crowd is they become the face of Christianity for scoffers – a clown's face. Those of us who are earnestly trying to be the hands, feet, and face of Christ in just and caring ways are then painted by the same dismissive brush. Guilty by association: *Christians*!

When Camping's prophesied end of the world came and went, a letter to the editor of *The Arizona Republic* jested, "I am a little disappointed that the world did not end on Saturday. I was kind of hoping that if all the religious fanatics went to heaven in the Rapture, we might get a little peace and quiet around here."

Years ago, Eric Swanson and Rick Rusaw, authors of *The Externally Focused Church*, asked, "If your church vanished, would your community weep? Would anyone notice? Would anyone care?"

Doomsday prophets, televangelists, and unscrupulous practitioners of the Christian faith may not be missed, but I submit there are Christians and congregations that would be. I'll venture a prophesy of my own: if Compton Heights Christian Church (Disciples of Christ) and Isaiah 58 Ministries were to vanish from 2149 S. Grand Blvd, St. Louis, MO, in the blink of eye, at the sound of the trumpet, raptured by the coming Christ, they would be missed. Absent the faithful of Compton Heights whose Sunday worship attendance hasn't crested 75 for four decades and absent the ministry to the community birthed with its ecumenical partners fifty-plus years ago, there would be grief.

After May 21, 2011, came and passed without the world's demise, Camping explained that a "spiritual" judgment had occurred on that date (whatever that means), but the "physical" end of the universe would take place on October 21, 2011. He suffered a stroke in June of 2011 and when his revised date of October 21, 2011, also came and passed, he retired from making predictions. Due to his failed "prophesies," his multi-million-dollar Family Radio empire declined precipitously. He died in December, 2013.

Compton Heights and Isaiah 58 ministries, however, live on. So do Millie and Barbara. No billboard. No radio show. No poofy hair or slick outfits. They quietly, humbly go about doing what they have always done, the one thing God requires: "Do justice, love mercy, walk humbly."

I'll prophesy once more. When God completes God's work and God's promised reign embraces the earth, Millie, Brenda, their staff and volunteers, and the Compton Heights folks will be lauded, "Well done, good and faithful servants."

Gold stamp it. GUARANTEED BY THE BIBLE.

Junior Detective

Urban ministry is not for the faint of heart. It can be tough: hard as asphalt. It can be trying: people in densely populated places can be ornery and obstinate. It can be costly: a drain on patience, compassion, and pocketbook.

One Sunday, I arrived at the church to find my office window air conditioner lying belly-up in the front yard, the window wide open. The following Thursday, one of the Day Care teachers arrived to open the building only to find that someone beat her to it – and beat in the back door and a few windows in the process.

I appointed myself junior detective. A VCR was gone. The window next to my desk was broken out. Beyond that, nothing was taken. The thief showed no interest whatsoever in the contents of a preacher's office. I was flummoxed.

All my books were in clear view, three shelves full, but not a single volume was taken. I counted 38 Bible dictionaries, books of worship, hymnals, Bibles, concordances, and lectionary aids. The thief bypassed them all. All 56 of my Bible commentaries offering verse-by-verse in-depth analyses of every book of the Bible (even Habakkuk and Obadiah) were untouched. Also left behind by the intruder were 42 theology books written by the likes of Tillich, Aquinas, Barth, Gutierrez, Schleiermacher, Calvin, and Finney. There was something for everyone on the theological spectrum. Augustine's 1,088-page *City of God* was there for the taking. The thief showed no interest. My 15 books on evangelism were accounted for, including a videotape on home calling techniques. You'd think that since the thief took the VCR, he'd also take something to watch on it.

Also left untouched: 30 books on church history, 20 on ethics (required reading for a thief), 12 books on stewardship (When he sold the VCR on the street would he tithe his take?), 47 books on prayer and spirituality (When he broke in and was sneaking through the church, I bet he was praying he wouldn't get caught), 27 books on pastoral care and counseling (Mr. Burglar, do you have a problem you'd like to talk about? I'm here to listen), a pile of visitor's packets and brochures welcoming folks to Compton Heights (Didn't he want to know more about the history, beliefs, and practices of the place he was breaking into?), and all my back issues of *Disciple* magazine (Now long out of print. Collector's items).

Neither did the prowler pilfer any of the 250+ sermons I had preached over the first half-dozen years of my ministry. Ok, I wasn't surprised by that. But he left behind two pictures I had on my desk of my two-year-old son (I thought everybody wanted one), the milk carton candle one of the youth in the Youth Group made me (There is none other like it. A Melvin original), and my robe and stoles (Probably didn't fit. I'm tall.) None of the above valuables were taken.

When you stop and think about it, a church is a lousy

place to break into. The most valuable thing in a church can't be taken, no matter how crafty the crook, it can only be received: the grace of God. It's freely available to all, even a petty thief (cf. Luke 23:32-43).

After my inventorying was complete, I closed my junior detective investigation and submitted a report to the board: The person who broke into the church didn't take anything of value. They were only looking for money and electronics.

Christmas Dinner

Nobody had to break into Compton Heights Christian Church. Our doors were wide open to everyone all week long and on Sundays, too. You never knew who would show up for worship. Take Grady, for instance, who bore a resemblance to Redd Foxx's friend named Grady on *Sanford and Son*.

Grady would amble in from time to time, help himself to some coffee, and talk to whoever happened to be nearby in an unintelligible gibberish, the product of misfitting teeth or none at all, I could never tell. He also had the rather disconcerting habit of kissing peoples' hands, or trying to anyway, in a manner that in nowise resembled the chivalrous gesture initiated by a woman of royal class offering her hand to a kneeling knight. Jennie and I were in the checkout line of the grocery store one day when Grady entered. Our cashier spotted him and said to a compatriot, "Oh no, not him!" Apparently, his reputation preceded him.

So it was that when Grady showed up for the Christmas Fellowship Dinner on the fourth Sunday of Advent, I saw a lot of hands shoved into pockets. People smiled at Grady, but they weren't extending the proverbial right hand of Christian Fellowship lest said hand be greeted by a not-so-holy kiss.

That Sunday, however, I watched as Grady used his own hands for a constructive purpose. He went from table to table, bussing people's plates. Working alongside him, bussing dishes five-at-a-time, was a member of Compton who had retired after years of waitressing. Think of Flo from *Mel's Diner* fame. Side-by-side with Grady, they bussed tables, their cumulative ages pushing one hundred and fifty years.

Flo asked, "Are you done with your meal?" "May we take your plate?" Whereupon Grady reached out, took the diner's plate, and walked it to the dishwashing area in the kitchen where Mary, Ella, and the Compton kitchen crew, aproned, hands elbow deep in suds, received his offerings with gratitude.

That morning in worship, we presented Bibles to Fentachew and Atseda, Ethiopian refugees who had fled to a refugee camp, then resettled in a neighborhood north of the church. The Bibles were in their native language of Amharic. Another Ethiopian family had been attending for several months. Millie and the Five Church Association staff had helped Assefa, Sinafkish, Behailu, Lydia, and Ayenew get settled months earlier with groceries and winter clothing. Cliff searched for jobs. We put out a call for used furniture and household goods. Raymond, a Five Church Association staffer whom I baptized, delivered the goods in FCA's van. Church members set up the apartment. I got my first taste of Immigration and Naturalization Services red tape helping Assefa apply for a visa for his wife so she could join him in St. Louis.

Lynwood, our choir director, donned a red elf's cap that drooped over his ears. He was playing Christmas carols when jovial Jim Clayton, decked out in a Santa outfit, entered with a bulging pillowcase slung over his shoulder. He was followed by several kids wearing brown construction paper antlers. Santa Jim pulled gifts wrapped in white tissue paper out of the pillowcase and handed them to the multiracial antlered reindeer who in turn placed them in front of the dinner guests.

One of the gifts got placed next to Fentachew and Atseda, evoking their second beaming smile of the day. Grady got one. Cathy, a developmentally disabled young woman befriended and brought to church by one of our young adult members received her gift and beamed. Four of our church's newlyweds, Tammy and Bill in their twenties and John and Ruby in their seventies were there, anticipating their first Christmas as husband and wife. They got gifts. Meanwhile, all three of the babies born that year, Nicole, Jessica, and Kira, were passed down the rows of seats from arm to arm, from one member of their church family to another. Black and white, young and old. Refugees from Ethiopia and lifelong St. Louisans. Lynwood in his elf cap, Jim in his Santa get-up, and the construction paper-eared reindeer. Flo and Grady bussing tables and carrying dishes to the rubber-gloved kitchen crew. Everybody went home with a gift that day, and not a one with a Grady hand kiss, which was a gift unto itself.

What It Takes to be a Saint

Mary and Ella, among the aproned, rubber-gloved kitchen crew for the Christmas Dinner, were two octogenarians tireless in their devotion to God and others. When I asked Mary what motivated her compassion and patience, she said, "I just tell myself, 'That's somebody's daughter. That's somebody's son.' Then I do for them what I'd want somebody to do for my son or daughter." Here's the thing: Mary didn't have any children. But God does, so all God's children became the recipients of Mary's loving largesse. She was a saint.

The Roman Catholic Church has a process of canonization. Following a five-year waiting period after the person dies, a bishop or other religious official can examine the virtue of the person and nominate them for sainthood as a "Servant of God." Next, The Congregation for the Causes of Saints reviews the candidate's life and, if warranted, refers the individual to the Pope who, if he finds "heroic virtue" may declare the person "venerable." To reach "beatification," evidence must be presented that shows a miracle took place as a result of prayers to the person. Canonization is the final rung on the ladder to sainthood, a status reached with evidence of a second miracle attributed to prayers made to the candidate after they have been beatified.

I respect my Catholic kin's criteria for sainthood, but this Protestant pastor has seen his share of people who, when the saints go marchin' in, most surely belong in that number. Mary is but one.

Paul's letters in the New Testament begin pretty much the same way. They read something like this:

From Paul, a servant of Jesus Christ, called to be an apostle. To all of you at the Christian Church in (fill in the city), all of you who are called to be saints. Grace to you and peace from God our Father and the Lord Jesus Christ.

Note the word *all* – "all of you who are called to be saints." That means you and me. According to Paul, we're *all* called to be saints.

So, what's it take to be a saint? Wings and a halo? Apparently not. Not one of the saints I've known in my lifetime had either. Let me tell you about some of the saints at Compton Heights and what it took for them to be saints.

I mentioned Mary above. Ella was Mary's sister in Christ and in service. She had neither wings nor a halo, but she had toenail clippers. You didn't know this until now, but to be a saint you need to have toenail clippers like the ones St. Ella had.

Ella's birthday was almost exactly fifty years before mine, so she sent me birthday greetings each year when the last week of September rolled around. She would also send me semi-monthly handwritten letters filling me in on how everybody in the congregation was doing. St. Ella visited Compton Heights members regularly. The hospitalized, homebound, broken-hearted, and lonely, Ella visited them. She said it was the least she could do for God – look after the old folks. Ella was in her late seventies when she said that.

Every few weeks, she'd go to nursing homes, kneel at residents' feet, and trim their toenails. When she told me that the first time, I scrunched my nose in disgust. Noticing the look on my face, she asked, "David, do you know the story about Jesus kneeling and washing his disciples' feet?"

I nodded my head.

"Well," she said, "Clipping toenails is the closest I can get to that."

Ella had neither wings nor halo, but she had toenail clippers. She had what it takes to be a saint.

But you don't need toenail clippers to be a saint. You just need orange, brown, black, and green construction paper. That's what St. Jerry had. St. Jerry was a ten-year-old who came to Compton. He and his sister Beverly were raised by their single mother, Barbara, a few blocks from the church. All three found a welcome in our midst.

Jerry had asthma. He got made fun of when he broke into a wheezing spell and got beat up by kids bigger and stronger than him. Every year, he spent several days at Cardinal Glennon Children's Hospital, a few blocks north of the church, getting his lungs working again.

Jerry was part of the Five Church Association youth group. Many had never ventured much beyond the Shaw Neighborhood. So, we'd load them into vans and take them on field trips. Expand their horizons. One December, we took them over the Mississippi into Illinois. Our Lady of the Snows, a shrine ten miles southeast of St. Louis, has an annual Way of Lights display, a drive-through retelling of the Christmas story, each scene illuminated with thousands of lights. After we had crossed the bridge and driven beyond the city lights into the country, Jerry pointed skyward out the window of the van and exclaimed, "Look, Pastor David! They have stars in Illinois!"

As a follow-up to the trip, we invited the youth to make Christmas cards. We set out construction paper, scissors, glue, glitter, and markers and let the youth have at it. Jerry cut out a green manger and an orange star, a black Mary and a brown Jesus. He glued them on a piece of construction paper which he folded in half. On the inside, he scrawled a message: *I hope all of you get better for Christmas. Love, Jerry.* He brought it to me and asked me to mail it for him.

"Where to, Jerry?"

"Cardinal Glennon Children's Hospital."

That Christmas, a card featuring a green manger, an orange star, a black Mary and a brown Jesus was received by the children at Cardinal Glennon compliments of St. Jerry. The boy had no wings, no halo, and sometimes no breath, but he had some construction paper and empathy – he had what it takes to be a saint.

To be a saint you don't even need to be able to cut and paste. St. Tiny had what it takes, and all he had was a pen and a piece of paper. Tiny and his wife Neva had been married for sixty-one years the day Tiny sat down to do something special for his beloved for their anniversary. Some folks are married for a long time, but they're no longer in love. They're just living together in wedlock. Then there are those who manage to stay in love. St. Tiny was among them. At age eighty-five or so and nearly blind, Tiny, a retired gas station attendant, sat down with a ballpoint pen in hand. He took a piece of paper and, with his hand shaking ever so slightly, wrote the most special thing he could think of: *I love you, Tiny*. Grown man. Married for ages. Still told his wife he loved her. That's why he's St. Tiny. His given name was Valentine.

St. Tiny was married to St. Neva. A crochet hook was her ticket to sainthood. Neva had terrible arthritis. I watched her use her left hand to open her right hand one finger at a time. Once open, she would place a pencil in it and reverse the process, closing her hand one finger at a time, wincing as she did, just to sign her name on a check for her and Tiny's offering on Sunday morning. When Jennie was pregnant with Will, our first child, Neva opened her arthritic hand, put a crochet hook in it, and started to make something. What it turned out to be was a large, colorful afghan she gifted to us at Will's birth. You've heard the expression labor of love. How many times did St. Neva have to open and close her hand around that crochet hook to put that afghan into our hands?

Then there was St. Lillian. One Sunday, Lillian ambled into the sanctuary mid-way through the announcements pushing her walker. Her son Walt or daughter Carol usually brought her to church, but they were out of town that weekend. Her granddaughter Kathy was there, though, and when she saw her grandmother come in, she gasped. After the service, she gasped again when she heard how her grandmother had gotten herself to church.

Somehow, St. Lillian had gotten up, gotten herself dressed,

eaten, taken her walker in hand and shuffled to the elevator, taken it down eleven floors, walked from the elevator to the front doors of the high-rise apartment building, and walked to the bus stop. When the bus arrived, she stepped off the curb and somehow got on the bus, paid the fare, and rode it two miles to the stop nearest the church. She managed to get off, stepped onto the curb, walked to the church, up the eight steps leading to the front door, got the door opened, and made it to her pew.

It is said, "The spirit is willing, but the flesh is weak." St. Lillian's flesh was no match for steps, curbs, blocks of city sidewalks, and a moving bus – but her spirit was bound and determined to worship God. Have walker, will worship!

What does it take to be a saint? Wings and a halo? A process involving bishops, the Pope, and authenticated miracles? How about toenail clippers or anything that'll help you serve another. Construction paper, or anything that'll help you tell someone else you care. A ball-point pen, a crochet hook, or anything that will spell out the words "I love you." A walker, a cane, your own two feet – whatever will get you to a place where you can worship God and have your Spirit refreshed and renewed. We have everything we need to be saints. All we need to do is use them.

From David, a servant of Jesus Christ, called to be a pastor. To all of you who are called to be saints. Grace to you and peace from God our Father and the Lord Jesus Christ.

The Acorn Does Not Fall
Far from the Tree

Mrs. Tarde's daughter and son, Carol and Walt, were among the saints of Compton.

Walt chaired the search committee that called me to Compton and, with his wife Audrey, remained a friend and encourager of my ministry over the next forty years. Carol was the guardian angel of Compton's ministry to the children and youth of the Shaw Neighborhood that stretched north, south, and west from the church. Jesus said, "Let the little children come to me, and do not hinder them, for the kingdom of heaven belongs to such as these" (Matthew 19:14). Jesus cribbed those words from Carol. Her tireless advocacy and unswerving support of the children and youth who found welcome and refuge at Compton were a wonder to behold.

Carol, assisted by a handful of other volunteers from the Five Church Association churches, directed the mother of all Vacation Bible Schools every July. The member congregations had few children and youth, so we reached out to the neighborhood around us and invited the neighbors' kids. They came. Over one hundred every year. And our four congregations, in a loaves and fishes kind of miracle, found enough willing and (sort of) able bodies to lead the program.

The adult-child ratio was about 25:1. It felt like 250:1 to those of us like Jennie and me who served as teachers and were assigned a passel of rambunctious, contentious, street-smart kids whose familiarity with things churchly and whose attention span in a cramped second floor classroom with no air conditioning was next to nil. To top it off, our VBS ran not from 9 a.m. - noon, but from 9 a.m. – 3 p.m. And not for one week, but three. I look back and wonder how we did it. It was Carol.

In his letter to the Corinthians, Paul listed things he'd been through during his ministry: "Imprisonments, count-less beatings, five times received the forty lashes less one, three times beaten with rods, stoned once, shipwrecked three times, adrift at sea for twenty-four hours, in danger from robbers, suffered many a sleepless night, constantly hungry and thirsty, often near death" (I Corinthians 11:23-37). Im-pressive. But did he ever go through three weeks of VBS?

I learned many things those years, including the fact that hot air really does rise, that a teacher's patience with ten-year-olds decreases as the temperature increases, that a ten-year-old's attention span decreases as the temperature increases, and that when a ten-year-old's attention span decreases, they will either squirm, pinch the kid sitting next to them, ask to get a drink, ask when it will be lunch time, or ask to go to the bathroom. With all those dynamics in mind, I knew I had about fifteen minutes each morning, a half-hour at most, to get in a few words edgewise about Jesus. During the other five and one-half hours of each day, my words about Jesus were limited to my pleading to him for patience, a cool breeze, and three o'clock.

Through it all, Carol remained what family systems therapist Edwin Friedman calls "a non-anxious presence." She was utterly unflappable. In Exodus, God is introduced as "Merciful and gracious, slow to anger and abounding in steadfast love" (Exodus 34:6). The child of God named Carol did not fall far from that tree.

What I never figured out as I reminisce about those yearly marathons is why I kept going back. Each year, right after the closing program, I'd vow to never do it again. I would put my foot down and make myself perfectly clear. "If nominated to teach VBS, I will not accept. If elected, I will not serve." Every year I said that and every year, come July, I'd find myself in the same sweltering room with two dozen ten-year-olds.

Likewise, throughout my forty years of ministry, I'd vow I'd done my time as a VBS teacher. Others can step up, I'd say. Then I'd think of Carol stepping up year in and year out. Or I'd think, I'm an empty-nester, old enough to be these kids' grandfather. And I'd think of Carol, graying hair in a bun, her warm, gentle smile radiating from her lovely visage. In my mind's eye I'd then see all the other VBS volunteers, veterans of innumerable mid-summer campaigns answering the call yet again, coming back for more. And I'd agree to do it again.

I know why I gave in. It never failed. At some point during the course of the week, in the midst of the construction paper and glue, the music and snacks, the prayers and pleas to use the bathroom, none other than Jesus Christ made an appearance at Vacation Bible School. Christ came. It never failed.

Those who take part year in and year out can testify to this phenomenon. And once he's come to you, you'll go through anything to encounter him again, be it shipwreck or imprisonment, be it beatings or sleepless nights … be it teaching Vacation Bible School to a slew of squirming children.

Enlisted again, I'd report for duty on the Monday morning of a new VBS. It wasn't dread; it was anticipation. It was adrenaline. It was Carol and people like her who, like Jesus, welcomed the children to come unto them. It was kids getting it at some precious moment, "it" being that they are Beloved in God's eyes, each gifted and graced and part of a family that transcended the brokenness many of them knew at home.

Just as her mother somehow made it to worship because it was Sunday morning, so Carol made it to VBS because it was July. Year in and year out she served until she died far too young of a heart attack.

Last summer, in the months leading up to my sixty-fourth birthday, I arrived in Columbia, MO, to begin an interim ministry. My first day coincided with their first day of VBS. Jennie and I did our part in memory of and thanksgiving for Carol.

But that was my last time … until next time.

The Lord's Latrine

Church camp counselor falls into the same category as Vacation Bible School volunteer in a pastor's job description, the one that reads, "and other duties as may be assigned." When I was a student ministerial intern at Central Christian Church (Disciples of Christ) in Danville, IL, during the summer of 1981, I was sent to be a camp counselor at Camp Walter Scott outside Effingham, IL. During my seminary years, my friend and colleague, Bob Hill, recruited me to serve alongside him for a week west of Nashville at Bethany Hills Camp. Compton Heights supported Orchard Crest, a camp 100 miles south of St. Louis outside Fredericktown, MO. Then followed stints at North Carolina's Camp Caroline and Christmount Christian Assembly, Indiana's Camp Bedford, and two camps in Arizona. When I arrived in Lexington at age fifty-five, my finicky back aggravated by rusty spring, worn-out mattress top bunks, I limited my participation in summer church camp to encouraging our children and youth to go, thanking our adult chaperones and counselors, and financially supporting the construction of a new bathhouse for the campers. My string of twenty-five summer counseling gigs was over.

But during those years, just as in VBS, there were moments that made the sleepless nights, refereeing middle school girls' drama, and calming homesick campers worthwhile.

I remember taking a bunch of ten-year-olds hiking through the far reaches of the woods. One of my ranks stopped dead in his tracks and called our attention to a six-foot-high fiberglass structure way off yonder. "Look! A refrigerator way out here in the middle of nowhere."

Before I could say a word, he dashed through the woods with half a dozen other campers in tow. They scampered up to the "refrigerator," grabbed hold of the latch, swung the door wide open, and got an up close and personal view and whiff of the inside of a latrine whose contents, by the look on their faces, scrunch of their noses, and howls coming out of their mouths, must have packed the potent olfactory punch of having been baked in the summer sun for several days undisturbed.

At the end of the week, when his parents came to pick him up, the first thing the leader of the pack did was lead them out to the back forty of the camp where he pointed out the latrine, informed them what it was there for, how it was used, and how it smelled. He was adamant about not opening the door.

After that show-and-tell, as they walked back to the camp, he told his parents how he was Joseph in the camp play. He whistled a song he learned around the campfire and handed his mother a prayer he wrote about God's good earth. He laughed as he told them about how one of his newfound friends had gotten poison ivy where the sun don't shine, on and on until he had pretty much rehearsed the entire week.

Summer church camp is a mixed bag. You laugh. You sing. You play. You pray. You discover new things like latrines that stink to high heaven and through it all, high heaven makes its way to earth, and kids walk away having met God.

It happened to Ken. He didn't seem to fit in at Camp Caroline, the North Carolina Region's campground for Disciples youth. On his first day, he showed up at the cabin next to mine, a boyish-looking freckle-faced redhead with a Pillsbury Doughboy build, squinting through his glasses, dragging a massive duffel bag. Under one arm, he held a diving mask and snorkel. In his free hand, he carried a pair of enormous flippers. Around his neck hung a powder blue camera. He paused outside the door to his cabin, dropped his flippers, lifted the camera to his eye, and with one hand snapped a picture. He then bent over, picked up the flippers, and proceeded into the cabin. That was my first impression of Ken.

Ken spent most of the week following the upperclassmen, a little boy tagging along at the heels of his big brothers, trying to fit in. Occasionally, he'd stop, lift the powder blue camera to his eye, snap a picture, and run to catch up with the pack. At best, his presence was tolerated by them. At worst, he was ignored.

Wednesday was the campers vs. counselors softball game. Ken came prepared. During warm-ups, he wore a red wristband on his glove hand and stood at second base ready to field a few grounders. The ball never came his way. He didn't make the starting lineup, so he sat on the bench snapping pictures with the powder blue camera. When the game was called due to darkness, he walked away toward his cabin with his head hung low.

I caught up with him, put an arm around his shoulder, and said, "Sorry you didn't get to play, Ken. Maybe we can work up another game later this week."

"No," he sighed, "that was the big game."

Thursday afternoon, Ken came up to me after quiet time in the cabin with a glimmer of brightness in his eyes. "Look what they did to me," he said, holding out his right hand. While Ken took an afternoon catnap, the older boys painted his fingernails with red nail polish. It didn't bother Ken, though. In fact, he seemed rather proud. They had shown him some attention.

Later, he came up to me, squinting, and said, "You know what they did to me now?" While he was sailing, one of the older boys had capsized Ken's boat, sending him into the drink. Ken came back up just fine, but his glasses didn't. Despite having lost them, he wasn't upset. He had been shown some attention.

I would have gone home feeling sorry for Ken were it not for the events of Friday night. There was a dance during which Ken stood in the shadows by himself swaying from side-to-side to the beat of the music (sort of). As the final song began, the youth circled up and began to dance together hand in hand. I saw two of the upperclassmen reach out to Ken. They took his hands in theirs and pulled him into the circle, put their arms around him, and danced to the beat of the music with Ken at their sides.

If I had Ken's powder blue camera, I would have snapped a picture. It would have shown Ken sandwiched between two upperclassmen, at long last welcomed and accepted, his face radiant.

Note to all who work with youth in the church: keep an eye peeled for the freckle-faced youth with the powder blue camera dangling around his neck, flippers under his arm, and a red wristband on his glove hand. You'll see him off to the side, hoping against hope that someone will notice him. Create a youth and children's ministry where no one will have to wait until the last dance to be invited in. If you do only that, you will have blessed somebody beyond measure, changed a life, and made a difference for the kingdom of God.

Urban Hobo

The wooded acreage of church camp was far removed from the concrete sidewalks and asphalt streets of the Shaw neighborhood Donald frequented on his bicycle.

I never knew his last name. I knew his first name only because every time he saw me, he extended his hand, saying, "Hey Preacher, how are you? Donald's the name." Then off he would go, sometimes unsteadily, up the stairs to the food pantry. I often had to escort Donald right back down the steps and out the front door with a gentle, yet firm admonition to come back when he sobered up. He'd come back a day or two later, smiling, hand extended, "Donald's the name."

Donald was, for all intents and purposes, a hobo. In an earlier era, Donald would have called the rail yards home. He would have hopped trains, slept in a rolling boxcar, and carried his worldly belongings in a bandana tied to the end of a pole slung over his shoulder. Cue Roger Miller's "King of the Road."

Absent trains to hop, Donald got a bicycle. It was an old red Schwinn with balloon tires. Every now and then, I spotted Donald peddling through the Shaw neighborhood wearing his floppy engineer's cap, sporting a Cheshire cat grin, one hand on the handlebar and the other holding a rake. He was an independent contractor of sorts. Leaf raking was his specialty, though he would do pretty much anything for a day's wage. Some folks on Flora Place took Donald under their wings, employing him regularly, so I saw him raking yards up and down the boulevard throughout the fall.

When June, Compton's secretary, spotted Donald ambling up the walkway to the church, she'd holler to me, "Here comes Donald!" I would in turn ring upstairs to the Five Church Association office, "Donald's on the way!" as if we were air traffic controllers tracking incoming aircraft. He'd enter with his mile-wide grin, extend his hand, say, "Hey Preacher, Donald's the name," and be on his way.

Sure, Donald could be a nuisance. Yet, there was something endearing about him. He was the big, playful mutt that shows up on the doorstep out of the blue. You feed him once out of sympathy, thinking he'll go on his way, but he jumps up and licks you profusely, big paws on your chest, tail wagging. You push him off and go back in but as he gallops off down the alley you hope he'll be all right ... and you're relieved when he shows up again a few days later. So it was with Donald. Word had it someone in the neighborhood let Donald store his beat-up balloon tire Schwinn in their garage for safekeeping, so he was endearing to others as well. Donald, the "have rake, will travel" urban hobo.

One fall, the leaves that fell on Flora Place were left for another's rake. Donald, last name unknown, was killed by a hit-and-run driver. One of the ladies on Flora Place whose leaves Donald raked was summoned to identify the body.

There were no known next-of-kin. He left behind a bicycle and rake.

Each year, as cooler temperatures arrive and leaves begin to fall, I think of Donald breezing through the neighborhood on his balloon-tired bike, grinning, rake slung over his shoulder. I think of the parable Jesus told about the king who hosted a banquet and invited the poor, the lame, and the blind (Luke 14:13-23). Surely Donald is on that invitation list to the heavenly feast. God knows his last name.

I smile as I envision him ambling up to the pearly gates (perhaps unsteadily) with rake slung over his shoulder, hand extended, saying, "Hey Peter, how are you? Donald's the name." Grinning. Welcomed. Redeemed. He rides through the gates atop his now shiny Schwinn, into his eternal inheritance.

Every Day is Gravy

Jack went to his eternal inheritance too soon. I had the privilege of knowing Jack McInnis for a few precious years and for that privilege I am grateful. His gap-toothed grin, soothing Mississippi drawl, and homespun sense of humor were endearing.

One summer day, I was processing the day's mail. The first handful of items I quickly tossed into the trash can. The last item in the pile, a succinctly written 3" x 5" postcard, I kept. The card read:

> *John D. McInnis, senior minister of First Christian Church, Jefferson City, MO, died early Sunday morning, July 3, of an apparent heart attack. A memorial service will be held at First Christian Church at 11 a.m., Thursday, July 7.*

I had been with Jack at a minister's retreat in Jefferson City a few months earlier. Chatting after one of the sessions, he told me of the heart attack that had nearly taken his life a few years earlier, the multiple bypass surgery that ensued, and his arduous recovery. I still recall the words with which Jack closed his recounting of that harrowing experience. I jotted them down in my journal for safekeeping. "After you've been through something like that," he said with his hands folded on his chest and his eyes gazing upward, "every day is gravy."

Why is it that it takes calamity, catastrophe, a brush with death, to remind us of the preciousness of life? Why do our senses become so dulled? It took the message on the postcard to remind me of the gift that is life. The Psalmist said, "This is the day that the Lord has made, let us rejoice and be glad in it" (Psalm 118:24). Every day. Grace-filled. God-given. Gravy.

At the end of Thornton Wilder's play *Our Town*, a young woman who died tragically in childbirth has an intimate conversation with the stage manager. The audience is privileged to eavesdrop on their exchange. The woman has been permitted a parting look at daily life in her small town. In a poignant final speech, she mourns the fact that she never fully enjoyed the small wonders of day-to-day living. Turning to the stage manager and audience, she says,

> *I didn't realize. So all that was going on and we never noticed. Take me back – up the hill – to my grave. But first: Wait! One more look. Good-by. Good-by, world. Good-by Grover's Corners … Mama and Papa. Good-by to clocks ticking … and Mama's sunflowers. And food and coffee. And new-ironed dresses and hot baths … and sleeping and waking up. Oh, earth, you're too wonderful for anybody to realize you.*

Then she looks toward the stage manager and asks through the tears, "Do any human beings ever realize life while they live it – every, every minute?"

The stage manager answers, "No." Then, after a pause, "The saints and poets, maybe – they do, some."

When I look back on that weekend at the retreat center, I realize I was in the presence of one who realized life while he lived it. Clocks ticking, sunflowers, food and coffee, hot baths, sleeping and waking up. Jack appreciated each one. For him, every day was gravy.

I vowed upon reading of his death and remembering his words that I would strive to awake each day to a posture of attentiveness, eyes wide open, soul receptive. I began a practice I have continued to this day, nearly forty years later. I bought a pack of index cards, one of which I carry in my pocket every day along with a pen. I jot down on the index card things I hear or see that shimmer – anything hinting of God, grace, or goodness. Likewise, when I hear something insightful, inspiring, provocative, or gospel true, I write it down. At the beginning of the next day, I enter my notations in my journal.

Through a process of trial and error that will soon turn forty, I developed a mission statement for my spirituality I have distilled into four words: I want to see, perceive, savor, and share.

See. The life of the Spirit begins with paying attention. In poet Mary Oliver's words, "Attention is the beginning of devotion." Frederick Buechner wrote,

> *Listen to your life. See it for the fathomless mystery it is. In the boredom and pain of it, no less than in the excitement and gladness: touch, taste, smell your way to the holy and hidden heart of it, because in the last analysis all moments are key moments, and life itself is grace.*

Burning bushes abound if we keep our eyes open. Prayer includes cupping our hands to our ears and listening closely, squinting through the eyes of faith and observing intently. Emily Dickinson: "The only commandment I ever obeyed – 'Consider the lilies.'" I want to pay attention to life.

Perceive. During my prayer time each morning, I look over the previous day's index card on which I wrote what I saw and heard in the hopes of perceiving connections and meaning. Mary Oliver again: "Do you think there is anything not attached by its unbreakable cord to everything else?" Each day is a string of pearls bound together by the thin thread of time. The pearls are the encounters, conversations, and observations that comprise a given day. When I take the time to stand back and look at – meditate on – what seem at first glance to be happenstance occurrences, something of meaning comes into focus. I perceive a truth. Glimpse grace. Hear the whisper of the Spirit. Jacob famously said upon arising from his dream of the ladder ascending into heaven, "Surely the Lord is in this place, and I did not know it" (Genesis 28:16). The fingerprints of Providence are on each day. I want to trace their outline, perceive what they are holding, offering, or pointing toward.

Savor. I want to take time each day to savor what I've seen and perceived. Savoring means everything from expressing gratitude ("Thank you, Lord") to being caught up in wonder (Mary Oliver for the third time: Our basic work in life is "learning to be astonished") to basking in the beauty of the arts or something beautifully said or done. Call it bourbon spirituality. Life is not meant to be gulped or consumed, but sipped, savored with appreciation for its many-splendored nuance. Thoreau went to the woods of Walden desiring "to live deep and suck all the marrow out of life." The word is savor.

Share. Having seen, perceived, and savored things, I want to share them so others may see and perceive what God is up to, savor it, and pass it on. For me, that sharing begins first thing each morning when I write in my journal. It ripples outward in conversations I have, in my teaching and preaching, and in the stories that have made their way into newsletter columns, articles, blog posts, and books.

Invariably, some of the best moments of my day are the ones spent in the morning reviewing and reliving the items on the previous day's index card. There's no telling how many index cards I've covered in scribble over the past four decades. Every one of them is splattered with gravy.

Father and Son

Jack died nine months after my father. Dad died just shy of his fifty-first birthday after a grueling three-year bout with cancer.

I spent my adolescence trying to excel in athletics in an effort to win his approval. In seventh grade, I tried out for the basketball team and was cut. In eighth grade, I tried out for the football team as a halfback and got flattened by defensive linemen who used me as a tackling dummy. I had my fill after two weeks. When I told Dad I had had enough, he took me out for lunch and gave me a lecture on how a Shirey never quits. I turned in my pads the next day.

That spring, I went out for the track team. No one got cut from the track team. I was too slow for the sprints and not agile or strong enough for the field events, so by a process of elimination, I ran the distance events. I didn't run fast enough in eighth or ninth grade to qualify for the meets, but as a sophomore I qualified for the two-mile run in the first meet of the year against our archrivals. My parents came to watch me. I moved to the front of the pack at the half-mile mark and stayed in the lead for the next mile and a quarter. I was in the lead at the start of the bell lap but was gassed. On the backstretch, two runners passed me. I held on for third, though. In my first high school meet, I scored a point for our team and went home elated.

I sat down at the dinner table smiling. But that countenance didn't last. I had no sooner pulled up my chair to the table than Dad asked, "Why'd you let those guys pass you?"

I snapped. "Never good enough, am I?"

Whereupon he slammed his hand on the table and yelled, "Go to your room!"

On the way out of the kitchen, I barked through clenched teeth, "Don't ever come watch me run again!"

He didn't. I lettered in cross country and track my sophomore, junior, and senior years of high school, ran occasional races during my college years and early adulthood, and have continued to run recreationally for the past four decades. Dozens of races. Thousands of miles. But because of that clash at the dinner table between a headstrong father and his headstrong son, he only saw me run once.

There is one other thing to which I have given myself with the discipline and passion I gave to running: preaching. Dad witnessed more than one of my sermons, not without some initial criticism. I preached my first sermon from the pulpit of Central Christian Church (Disciples of Christ) in Warren, OH, on Youth Sunday in 1975. I was sixteen years old. My topic was "God is love." Dad's remark afterward was, "You talked too fast." He was right. My stomach was in knots and my knees were trembling. It was all I could do to read the manuscript in front of me.

In the summer of 1981, between my graduation from Indiana University with a Religious Studies degree and my first year at Vanderbilt Divinity School, I was a student minister at Central Christian in Danville, IL. I preached sermons 2 through 5 there. Dad was there for all of them. Not a churchgoer, his presence in worship on those Sunday mornings rather than on the golf course was not lost on me. Neither was it lost on me that he didn't say anything critical after any of them.

Though present for sermons 1 through 5, Dad didn't hear numbers 6 through 256. Those five years' worth of sermons were preached during my three years at Carthage Christian Church and during my first two years at Compton Heights. While I was acclimating myself to the pulpit in Carthage, he and Mom were travelling to cancer wards as far away as Boston. He was beginning yet another round of chemotherapy when I was ordained in May of 1985, so my aunt and uncle represented my family that day. It was off to St. Louis after that, but as the cancer become more aggressive and Dad became weaker, a three-hour drive from Danville to St. Louis was out of the question. Jennie and I made regular four hundred-mile roundtrips to visit in 1985 and, after our son Will was born in 1986, we continued those road trips to place twelve-month-old Will in his grandfather's frail arms.

Easter Sunday, 1987. Dad woke my mother in the middle of the night and said, "Drive me to St. Louis. I want to hear David preach." Disoriented by being wakened at that hour as well as by Dad's unprecedented request, my mother asked how she was going to transport his bedridden body on a three-hour drive.

"Call Ron," Dad said, referring to a family friend. "Tell

him we're borrowing his van." The plan was for Dad to lie down on a pallet in the back of the van with my mother on nursing duty in one of the Captain Chairs. My brother, twenty-three at the time, had gotten home at 2 a.m. after having spent the night doing who knows what. He was awakened at 5 a.m. by Mom with the summons to chauffeur duty.

I knew nothing of their coming until I processed down the aisle singing "Christ the Lord Is Risen Today," pivoted at the chancel, looked out over the congregation, and saw the gaunt man in the second pew from the pulpit wearing a collared shirt too big for his thinning neck, a poorly knotted tie hanging limply down his front. He looked up at me through tired gray eyes, his mouth turned up ever so slightly. A smile?

It's hard to sing "Alleluia" with a lump in your throat.

When I preached, he fixed his eyes on me. When the communion bread and cup were passed, he participated. When the service was over, he slowly rose to his feet and walked gingerly to where I was greeting worshippers at the front door. He looked me in the eye and extended his hand. Though he said not a word, what I understood loud and clear by his handshake and his visage that transcended that scourge cancer was, "I'm proud of you." At long last, I had received my father's blessing.

As he was being helped into the van by my bleary-eyed brother and me, Dad said he wanted to take his fourteen-month-old grandson home with him for a few days. We strapped Will's car seat in one of the Captain Chairs in front of Dad's pallet and waved as they pulled away from the curb and headed back to Danville.

That was the last time Dad would attend a worship service. It was the sixth and last of my 2,000+ sermons he would hear. He died five months later on my twenty-eighth birthday. Each year since, on the date of my birth and his death, I remember his visit, visage, and unspoken affirmation, and receive them with gratitude for the gift they were … and still are.

Now when I think of my father, I do not remember him at the kitchen table asking why I let those two runners pass me, the day that divided us. Rather, I remember him in the second pew, leaning in and listening to the promises of the resurrection, the day that united us … and still does.

Kneeling

When I was growing up, I had a choice to make every Sunday. I could go to church with Mom at Central Christian or stay at home and work around the house with Dad. In my childhood and early adolescence, going to church with Mom was the lesser of two evils.

When I was seventeen, a rising senior in high school, my parents moved from Ohio to Illinois. I wanted to finish high school in Warren, OH, where I was born and raised, so I lived with my grandparents. No sooner had my family pulled out of the driveway on their move west than my grandmother laid down the house rules. When she got to the subject of churchgoing, she said, "David, church is up to you. You're a young man. Decide for yourself. If you want to go with Poppy and me to Emmanuel Lutheran, we go to the eight o'clock service. You need to be ready by twenty 'til. *That wasn't happening.* If you want to go to Central Christian, you can drive yourself in Poppy's car. If you don't want to go at all, you don't have to. It's up to you."

I sat on my twin bed in my makeshift room in their basement weighing my options. Why did I go to church? Did I go because it was the lesser of two evils? Did I actually believe something? I wasn't sure.

I decided I needed to pray about it. But there was one problem: I didn't know the first thing about prayer. I did have a notion, however, that if I wanted to pray, there was a proper posture – kneeling. So, I got down on my knees at the side of my twin bed in the basement. My elbows propped on the mattress, my hands folded in front of me, I said something like, "God, if you're there. I want to know." At that very moment (drum roll please), my grandfather flushed the upstairs toilet. There was no rending of the heavens. No descent of the heavenly dove. Just a flush and whoosh from the plumbing on high.

I got up the next Sunday and went to church by myself. Why? Because there were people at Central Christian who knew me by name, who spoke to me when I was there and expressed an interest in me, people I would miss if I didn't go to church. I'd go because of them. The God part I could figure out in time. Such was my seventeen-year-old reasoning.

Several summers ago, I was back at Central Christian for the first time in thirty-five years. I walked in, took a seat halfway back, and looked out over a sparse congregation of people I didn't recognize. Then I saw Mr. Hawn. I watched as he worked his way through the pews greeting people. When he made it to where I was sitting, he looked at me, paused, and said, "Dave Shirey!"

I said, "No way! Thirty-five years later and you remember me?"

After church, I told him, "I want you to know that back when I wasn't sure why I came to church, when I wasn't sure what I believed about God, you were one of the reasons I decided to keep coming. I owe you a debt of gratitude."

Eleven years after I knelt in my grandparents' basement, I got on my knees again. I had returned to St. Louis after Dad's death. I was physically and emotionally exhausted, which I attributed to grief. But I was spiritually empty as well. I made a diagnosis. After a long, hard look at my soul's fuel gauge reading E, I gave myself an F for not knowing how to pray. Not knowing what else to do, I did what I had done in my grandparents' basement. I knelt beside the desk in my office and prayed.

"Lord, I know there's more than this. I'm doing a lot of talking *about* you but not *to* you or *with* you. My faith is secondhand rather than first-person. I can *say* prayers and *write* prayers, but I'm not a prayerful person. Prayer is in my tool belt as a pastor, but it's not woven into the fabric of my life. Teach me to pray."

A scripture came to mind. Acts 2:42 reads, "And they devoted themselves to the apostles teaching and fellowship, to the breaking of the bread and the prayers."

The gist of what I sensed the Spirit whisper to me was, "The word is devoted, David. They devoted themselves to poring over Scripture and praying. They intentionally spent time together over meals grappling with matters of faith and life. You're not devoted yet. You're just dabbling. If you want to take the next step, when you wake up tomorrow morning, grab your Bible and a notebook and give me a call. I'll speak to you through Scripture. Write down what you think you're hearing in a journal. Prayer is what that is – Me talking. You listening, reflecting, and responding. Make that a daily habit and leave the rest to me. Our relationship will change and so will you."

It wasn't like I was taking dictation as God spoke. It was an inaudible whisper, what Elijah experienced as a "still, small voice" (1 Kings 19:12), a communication of a different order than a toilet flushing.

I began the next day what has become a daily habit of setting aside time each morning to pray and journal. I began to learn what it means to be a prayerful person, what Paul meant when he said, "Pray without ceasing" (1 Thessalonians 5:17). I crossed the threshold that leads from a second-hand to a first-person relationship with God. For the last I-don't-know-how-many-years, Laura, my youngest daughter, has given me the same Christmas present: a new prayer journal for the coming year. I have dozens of them in the closet of my study. It all started that afternoon in 1987 when I knelt deskside at Compton Heights.

Fast forward twenty years from St. Louis. In 2007, Jennie and I were five years into planting a new church from scratch in the desert northeast of Phoenix. I was studying the story of David and Goliath in 1 Samuel 17:40. Shepherd boy David knelt at the brook to fetch five smooth stones with which to do battle with fearsome Goliath. In his reflection on the David and Goliath story in his masterful book about David titled *Leap Over a Wall*, the late Eugene Peterson wrote: "Are we going to live this life from our knees ... or ... are we going to be shaped by our fears of Goliath?"

That question became a living and active word to me, namely: King David lived life from his knees. Will David Shirey live life from his knees?

I sent an email to a member of my congregation who was a woodworker. "Paul, would it be possible for you to build me a prayer bench? I can describe for you what I have in mind. Nothing fancy. Just something I kneel on when I pray. I could show you some pictures as examples."

The next day I received a message from Paul. "Pastor, 'Ask and ye shall receive.' I have a beautiful prayer bench at my house that would be blessed by your continuous use. It is a design that I had in my head for years and finally with much coaxing from my friend, James, he and I built it a year and a half ago with the hopes it would help ease all the trials that he, Tracey, and the girls have been through. It is made of solid maple and has a nice neutral-toned tapestry print on the kneeler and armrest."

The next day, Paul dropped off a kneeler that was in my Phoenix home from 2008 until Coolwater Christian Church's first building was constructed in 2011. From that day on, it was in the anteroom to our sanctuary, a room we dubbed the Prayer Chapel. I went into that room every Sunday before the service started, knelt at the bench, and prayed. Throughout the week, I made my way to that kneeler as needed, which was often.

I'm thinking of other seasons of my life when I knelt.

In 1989, when trying to discern whether I was being called to a church in North Carolina that was outside my comfort zone (stretched again), I knelt.

In 2001 in Indiana, when I was wrestling with whether to submit my resignation with nowhere to go, I knelt.

During the dozen years Jennie and I were planting the church from scratch, sowing gospel seeds in parched desert soil from 2002-2014, I knelt.

The search committee of historic Central Christian Church in Lexington, KY, flew me to Lexington in the spring of 2014 to interview. I asked for some private time in the sanctuary. I sat in the front pew and prayed for a while. Then I knew what I needed to do. I got up, walked forward, and knelt on the chancel steps in front of the communion table.

I look back to the progression of asks I have made while kneeling, beginning with "God, are you there?" and continuing through "Teach me to pray" and "Am I being called to move 1,800 miles from the desert to the Bluegrass?"

The wonder of it all is that prayer, the vitalizing taproot of my life, came to me in the wake of my father's death. He was not a man of faith. Ours was a relationship that never quite jibed. But D. Keith Shirey bequeathed to me in his dying the spiritual inheritance that has most impacted my living. Jack's death gifted me with the index cards. Dad's death taught me to pray.

Why?

It's one thing to kneel in supplication before God of your own volition. It's another to be brought to your knees, befallen by tragedy. Every pastor has received the late-night call, harbinger of a halting communication delivered through a constricted throat. Then follows the hastening to the hospital, house, or scene where a life is in the balance or has ended, sometimes unexpectedly, prematurely, or violently. Then ensues keeping vigil in mute solidarity with those in the excruciating grip of raw grief.

Within a year of my arrival at Compton Heights, I was initiated into the circle of crisis caregiving. I was summoned to St. Louis University Hospital where, in a tiny windowless room demarcated *Family Consultation Room*, I huddled with a woman whose eldest son, a young man my age, mid-twenties, had been killed in a fight outside a bar. In my journal, I noted "long periods of silence, intermittent embraces, and inconsolable sobs. Few words were exchanged."

A few months later, I received a call from our music director. Her son, also my age, had been killed in a car accident.

Then a call from one of our deacons. His sixty-six-year-old wife, having struggled with depression, had taken her own life with a firearm. Quinton got home from work, found Helen in their bedroom, and made two calls – the first to 911, the second to me. The first responders were just leaving. Would I please come? Though Helen's body had been removed when I arrived, the wall of their bedroom bore her lifeblood. Quinton and I stood together mute, my arm around his shoulder as much to support myself as to support him.

Those three deaths ushered me into ministry in the face of tragedy, a threshold over which every pastor must cross innumerable times in ministry. Each occasion seared on our memories. The circumstances indelibly etched. The memory of how we tried to compose ourselves en route to the place of meeting. The clearing of the throat before knocking on the door. A deep breath. The opening of the door. Your eyes meeting theirs. Your presence evoking a wave of emotion. The extending of arms opened wide. The leaning toward another.

It's not what you say in such moments, Liston Mills, my professor of pastoral care, taught us, it is who you are: a pastor. Their pastor. You needn't *say*, just *be*.

"I'm so sorry," were the words I whispered.

"Why?" asked the woman whose son was killed in the bar fight. It was not a question she was expecting me to answer as much as a reflexive, inchoate gasp.

Why? Grappling with that question ushers one into the realm of theodicy. *Encyclopedia Britannica* defines the word: "Theodicy, (from Greek *theos*, "god"; *dikē*, "justice"), explanation of why a perfectly good, almighty, and all-knowing God permits evil. The term literally means 'justifying God.'"

The logic that informs the theodicy conundrum is as follows:

- *If God is all-good, then God has the desire to end suffering.*
- *If God is all-powerful (omnipotent), then God has the ability to end suffering.*
- *If God does not end suffering, then God is either not all-good or not all-powerful.*

Philosophers and theologians have waxed eloquently on the subject of theodicy for centuries. My bookshelf included Phillip Yancey's *Where is God When It Hurts?*, Adam Hamilton's *Why?*, Rabbi Harold Kushner's bestselling *When Bad Things Happen to Good People*, and Nicholas Wolterstorff's *Lament for a Son*. Wolterstorff and Kushner wrote their books after the tragic deaths of their sons, the former to a tragic accident and the latter to a rare disease. Hamilton wrote his after his youth pastor and the pastor's brother died within minutes of each other after an accident.

At some point, *Why?* becomes personal for us all. The word theodicy may not be familiar, but its generative cause is: the sting of death.

What follows is a sermon that was preached a few years after I faced the incidents I recollected at the outset of this chapter and others of their painful kind that followed. By then, I was no stranger to the sting of death and the question *Why?* What provoked the sermon were all the answers posited to the *Why?* question that I had read or heard (and I dare say, may have spoken) that were unsatisfactory at best or woefully inappropriate, even hurtful, at worst.

I do not purport to offer an answer. I present what follows

to honor the memory of the precious souls in my congregations whose dying evoked the late-night calls, the keeping of silent vigil, the "I'm sorry" whispered in compassionate embrace. To borrow words from 1 Peter 3:15, these sermons represent my effort "to give an accounting for the hope that is within me."

***

Why? – a sermon

In 1981, a book rose to the top of the *New York Times* bestseller list. *When Bad Things Happen to Good People* was written by Rabbi Harold Kushner following the death of his fourteen-year-old son from a rare aging disease called progeria. Many people misread the title. They thought it was *Why Bad Things Happen to Good People* and read it hoping the rabbi would provide the definitive answer to the age-old question of *Why?* If God is great and God is good, then why is there suffering? Where is God when it hurts?

I don't pretend to have an answer. I do, however, have a short list of popular answers that I no longer find either helpful or biblical, though earlier in my life I thought they were both. They include the phrases, "It must be God's will," "There's a reason for everything," and "God won't put on you more than you can bear."

I remember the circumstance that forced me to wrestle with these responses to suffering and others like them. In 1983, I was serving as a hospital chaplain in Nashville, TN. I befriended a middle-aged woman whose mother was hospitalized with an incurable heart disease. One day I saw her standing at a window at the end of the hallway, lost in thought. As I came up next to her, I saw tears streaking her cheek.

"Your mother?" I asked.

"No," she said, "My daughter. Yesterday she gave birth to my first grandchild. A girl. She was stillborn."

I said, "I'm so sorry."

To which she responded, "It must be God's will. There's a reason for everything. He won't put on us more than we can bear." She said those phrases in an emotionless monotone. It was as though she was saying things she thought she was supposed to say as a woman of faith, but she didn't believe them.

I went back to my apartment and did some soul-searching.

She said, "It must be God's will." I wondered: Really? Can an elderly woman's suffering, a young mother's unspeakable grief, and a middle-aged woman's anguish really be a good and loving God's will – God's intention and desire for people God loves?

I remembered a story Leslie Weatherhead, a British pastor, told in his book, *The Will of God*, about a friend whose son died in a cholera epidemic in India. When the man said, "It's the will of God," Weatherhead said to him, "John, suppose someone crept up the steps onto the veranda tonight while you all slept and deliberately put a wad of cotton soaked in cholera germ culture over your little boy's mouth as he lay in that cot over there sleeping. What would you think about that?"

He responded, "Nobody would do such a damnable thing. If he did and I caught him, I'd kill him as I would a snake and throw him over the veranda. What do you mean by suggesting such a thing?"

Weatherhead said, "Isn't that what you've just accused God of doing when you call it his will that your boy died of cholera?"

He wrote, "In no way can it be God's intention to pour misery undeserved and unhappiness, disappointment and frustration, bereavement, calamity, and ill health on his beloved children, and then ask them to look through their tears and say, 'Thy will be done.' Such things cannot be the intentional will of the God we know through Jesus Christ."

I thought to myself: If it's God's will that the woman's mother suffer and die as well as her firstborn grandchild, does that mean that all the cardiologists' efforts to fight her mother's heart disease and the obstetric team's months-long effort to bring her daughter's pregnancy to term and all my intercessory prayers for life and health were *contrary* to the will of God? Surely not. That makes no sense.

But whether or not it made sense to claim those tragedies were somehow the will of God, the woman had also said, "There's a reason for everything." The implication is everything happens the way it does because it's God's will for it to happen that way. Nothing happens without God causing it or allowing it to happen. So, if it happens – if suffering happens – the reason is God. Or as someone said, "God has his reasons and your common sense can't always make sense of God's Uncommon Sense."

I respectfully object. I know Isaiah reminds us, "My thoughts are not your thoughts, neither are your ways my ways, says the Lord" (Isaiah 55:8). But I can't believe that in order to accomplish loving *ends* God would intentionally employ hurtful, heart-breaking *means*. I can't bring myself to say "There's a reason for everything" if what is implied is that God has some Master Plan beyond my understanding for which the awful things that happen to people are somehow the tools God uses to accomplish it.

Now, if by saying "There is a reason for everything" what is meant is there is a cause behind every effect, I believe that. I believe the reason for my father's cancer and death at age fifty-one was his thirty-year two-pack-a-day smoking habit. The reason for the tragic death of so many lives each year on our nation's highways is people horribly abusing their free will by drinking and driving. The reason for a plane's crashing and two hundred fifty passengers' lives being lost is a malfunction in the engine or wind shear. The reason for tornados is an atmospheric collision of hot and cold air masses. But to imply that such things as natural disasters and mechanical malfunctions, abuses of free will, and poor lifestyle choices are orchestrated by God – that the reason for everything, including every bad thing, is God – I can't accept that.

The woman at the hospital in Nashville also said, "God won't put on you more than you can bear." I used to say those words. But then I asked myself: Do I really believe God puts suffering on people – though not more than we can bear? Did God put on that woman the responsibility of her mother's care? Seeing that she was handling that without breaking, did God then "put" on her the death of her granddaughter and the grief of her daughter? Since she was still standing after that, might God have put more on her? We call people who intentionally afflict other people with suffering "sadists" and those who accept such affliction "masochists." I wouldn't use either word to refer to God or people of faith.

I looked up the phrase "God won't put on you more than you can bear" in the Bible. I found it in 1 Corinthians 10:13. But I found that the phrase has nothing to do with suffering and everything to do with temptation. The Scripture reads, "God … will not let you be tempted beyond your strength, but with the temptation will also provide you the way of escape, that you may be able to endure it" (1 Cor 10:13). Bottom line: saying "God won't put on you more than you can bear" is appropriate if you're struggling against temptation, but out of context if used to explain suffering.

I thought of that dear woman looking out that window with tears streaming down her face saying, "It must be God's will. There's a reason for everything. He doesn't put on us more than we can bear." I disagree.

To which I imagined her say in response, "Then where is God right now, Chaplain? Where is God when it hurts?"

I can only share what I believe.

I believe God is present to comfort those who suffer. Psalm 55:22 promises, "Cast your burden on the Lord and he will strengthen thee." As opposed to God's casting or putting burdens on us, Jesus said, "Come unto me all ye who are weary and heavy laden and I will give you rest" (Matthew 11:28). Jesus' last words to his disciples in Matthew 28 were "I will be with you always." Especially when we suffer.

I believe God is actively at work to overcome the sources of and reasons for suffering. Everything from viruses to villains – whatever conspires to cause suffering – God is actively working to subdue. The opening chapters of Genesis present God as bringing order out of chaos. To me, that translates to

God always seeking to bring healing out of suffering, solace out of grief, life out of death. That Jesus' ministry involved exorcising evil, healing the sick, and raising the dead assures me God is ever battling the sources of suffering.

I believe God is able to redeem suffering. God doesn't will bad things to happen, but when bad things happen, God wills and works for the good. God doesn't cause bad things. God does work to redeem us from them. At the heart of our faith is God's taking a cross – "the emblem of suffering and shame"– and turning it into an instrument of salvation. In the words of Frederick Buechner, "Resurrection means the worst thing is never the last thing." The Psalmist says, "O Israel, hope in the Lord! For with the Lord there is steadfast love, and with him is great power to redeem" (130:7).

I believe God will ultimately prevail over suffering. Someone pointed out to me long ago that though many psalms begin in suffering and pain, they end in praise. And they pointed out that though what are called the lament psalms are more numerous than what are called the psalms of thanksgiving and trust, the latter psalms, and the last five in particular, are undiluted praise and thanksgiving. Meaning what? Meaning the Psalms invite us to believe that no matter what we are facing now, by God's grace and God's help, laments will ultimately be turned to praise: "Those who go out weeping … shall come home with shouts of joy" (Psalm 126:6).

The late William Sloane Coffin lost a son in a tragic automobile accident. Driving in a terrible storm, Alex's car slid off the road into Boston Harbor where he drowned. In a sermon Dr. Coffin preached after the tragedy, he said, "My own consolation lies in knowing that it was not the will of God that Alex die; that when the waves closed over the sinking car, God's heart was the first of all our hearts to break." In his long season of mourning, he prayed the lament Psalms and noted something to which he held fast throughout his grief. In his words, "The psalm that begins, 'My God, my God, why hast thou forsaken me' only begins that way, it doesn't end that way."

The age-old question in the face of suffering is Why?

I don't believe suffering is God's will or that the reason for suffering is God or that God puts on us things no one ought ever have to bear.

I do believe God is "a very present help in times of trouble" (Psalm 46:1).

I do believe God has "great power to redeem" (Psalm 130:7).

I do believe that one day God will "wipe away every tear from our eyes. Death will be no more, neither shall there be mourning nor crying nor pain any more" (Psalm 21:4).

These things I believe and you can believe them, too, when bad things happen to good people.

Let all God's people say, AMEN.

Orientation: Joyful

Don faced his death with resolute joy. He grew up at Compton Heights, graduated from Bethany College, felt a call to ministry, and went to Yale Divinity School. After he was ordained, he served as Associate Minister at First Christian in St. Joseph, MO, pastored First Christian in Cape Girardeau, MO, then went to First Christian in Columbia, MO, where he had responsibilities in campus ministry, membership, community action, and outreach. When I arrived in 1985, Don was pastoring a house church in St. Louis. Circle of Life was composed of a few dozen folks seeking a place of welcome and belonging outside the walls of the church.

Don, too, sought that welcome and belonging. Don was gay.

In 1993, President Bill Clinton ushered in legislation dubbed "Don't Ask, Don't Tell" under which homosexuals serving in the military were not allowed to talk about their sexual orientation and commanding officers weren't permitted to question service members about it. Though Clinton's intention was to provide a way for gays and lesbians to serve in the military, it was far from acceptance. Military personnel were mandated to keep their identities secret in exchange for offering their lives in service to their country. An equitable exchange?

The church was years behind the military when it came to its enlisted personnel. Everyone conspired to silence regarding beloved, gifted pastors, Christian educators, music directors and organists who were lifelong bachelors or bachelorettes. Didn't ask. Didn't tell. Didn't dare. People can be so mean. Christians can be so cruel.

During my years at Compton Heights, resolutions were brought to our denomination's biennial General Assembly that reflected society's conflicted coming to terms with the sexual orientation of people who identify as LGBTQIA+. In 1987, the General Assembly rejected a resolution brought by conservative delegates calling homosexuality sinful. In 1989, delegates approved a resolution calling on the church and its members to treat persons with AIDS as children of God and to "act as instruments of God's compassionate love and tender care when the seeds of fear, prejudice, and alienation have been sown." Though Don was a delegate at the 1987 Assembly and able to cast a vote in favor of his self-worth as a human being created in the image of God, he was not present for the 1989 General Assembly. Diagnosed with pancreatic cancer in the summer of 1988, he was rail thin by Advent of that year. Jaundiced. Dying. He died in 1989, but not before preaching a sermon on joy using only a candlelighter and Christmas carol.

Our worship committee chose folks to light the Advent wreath. When they handed me the list for Advent 1988, I looked at it and said, "You asked Don to light the Advent wreath on the Third Sunday of Advent? That's the Joy candle. Don's dying. What were you thinking?"

They said, "He said he'd do it."

I said, "I'll go by and talk to him."

There was nothing to talk about.

"David," he said, "I know it's the Joy candle. That's the one I want to light."

The scripture that Sunday was Philippians 4:4-9. Paul wrote, "Rejoice in the Lord always." Mind you, he was in a Roman jail cell. How could he rejoice? He lifted his head and hands and rejoiced when he ought to have buried his head in his hands and sighed. How can that be?

What that says to me is joy – biblical joy – is not dependent on external circumstances, but upon an awareness of God's presence in all circumstances. In Barbara Brown Taylor's words, "The only condition for joy is the presence of God. Joy happens when God is present and people know it."

The fact that joy transcends circumstances is a blessed truth I'm reminded of whenever I hear the spirituals. Michael Curry, Presiding Bishop of the Episcopal Church, a black man whose faith was forged by the spirituals, wondered, "Why didn't slaves go crazy? They had no doctors, no therapists or social workers. Families were separated and sold." He says, "I believe it was their singing. Spirituals took away their shame, wiped away their tears and made them part of God's own family." Nobody and nothing was going to steal their joy! Paul rejoicing in prison and slaves singing in the fields beneath their taskmasters' noses bear witness to a truth fundamental to faith: joy transcends circumstances. If God is near, joy will find a way.

Paul continued his ode to joy by testifying, "I've learned in whatever state I am to be content. I've learned how to be abased and how to abound; in any and all circumstances I have learned the secret of facing plenty and hunger, abundance and want. I can do all things through Christ who strengthens me" (Philippians 4:11-13).

The word *content* is from a Medieval Latin word that means "held together." When Paul said, "I've learned in whatever state I am to be content," he was saying, "No matter what, I trust my life will be held together by God."

Have you ever noticed the word *religion* has in its center the letters l-i-g – lig – as in the word *ligament*. What does a ligament do? It holds us together, connects bone to bone. The spiritual "Dem Bones" sings, "The toe bone's connected to the foot bone/ The foot bone's connected to the ankle bone/ The ankle bone's connected to the shin bone." Ligaments hold our bodies together. Religion at its best holds everything together: ligs us to each other, God, and all creation. Religion at its best isn't a five-inch-thick dictionary of dogma – things you must believe – or a rulebook of things you'd better do or not do. Re*lig*ion as in *lig*ament is a way of living life that strives to hold relationships, societies, and creation together. Give me some of that 'ol time religion Paul had, born of his conviction that the Lord was near, holding him together, filling him with joy and a "peace that passes understanding."

I'll never forget Don processing down the center aisle that Third Sunday of Advent as we sang the opening hymn. He walked unsteadily, his face gaunt. As he reached the front of the sanctuary, his back to the congregation, his face toward where I stood on the chancel, the flame of the candlelighter he held before him bathed his jaundiced face in a soft glow. I remember the look on his face – a peace that passes understanding; a radiant, intrepid joy. Having lit the Joy candle, he turned, faced the congregation he had grown up in as a child and returned to at the end of life, and said, "Joy to the world, the Lord is come. Let earth receive her king. Let every heart prepare him room, and heaven and nature sing." With that, he solemnly, a bit unevenly, returned to his pew, the candle softly burning – Joy. Joy. Joy.

Don stopped by my office a few days before Christmas with a present – a homemade ornament he had crafted. It is a 5" high right-angled triangle made out of powder blue cardstock, a circular hole punched at the tip through which Jennie looped and tied string so we could hang it on our tree. On one side, at the top of the triangle, Don drew a shimmering star with a deep blue colored pencil. Emanating from it toward the tip and in long strokes to the base are rays of orange, blue, and yellow. On the flip side, also of Don's craftsmanship, is a quartet of free verse poetry in his crisp, elegant handwriting that reads:

His beginning is storied
Mine I can't recall
But I see tomorrow
All entries & exits integrated
    DGP '88

The ornament, its radiant starlight on one side and radiant verse on the other prophesying the ultimate holding together of all things – "All entries & exits integrated" – reminds me each Christmas of the man whose visage yet shimmers in my memory.

I led Don's funeral nine weeks after he lit the Joy candle. It was a Saturday in February, the dead of winter. Members of his Circle of Life congregation were there mourning their pastor and friend. Members of his home church were there hosting the service. Together we mourned one of our own, a pastor, a brother in Christ, a child of God, a man beloved.

The previous fall, Don handed me an envelope. Inside, in the same indelible handwriting that inscribed the Christmas ornament, were his desires for his funeral, which we honored.

The Prelude was J.S. Bach's "Jesu, Joy of Man's Desiring."

The Call to Worship was a responsive reading Don crafted from Psalm 130:

Out of the depths I cry to thee, O Lord!
    Lord, hear my voice!
Let thy ears be attentive to the voice of my supplications:
    I wait for the Lord, my soul waits, and in God's
    word I hope.
O Israel, hope in the Lord!
    For with the Lord there is steadfast love,
    With our God there is plenteous redemption.

Selections of poetry and the Beatitudes were read.

We sang "Blest Be the Tie That Binds," followed by a reading from Psalm 27:

The Lord is my light and my salvation;
    whom shall I fear?
One thing have I asked of the Lord,

that will I seek after;
that I may dwell in the house of the Lord
   all the days of my life,
to behold the beauty of the Lord,
   and to inquire in his temple.
I believe that I shall see the goodness of the Lord
   in the land of the living!
Wait for the Lord;
   be strong, and let your heart take courage;
   yea, wait for the Lord!

Also, Psalm 139:

Whither shall I go from thy Spirit?
   Or whither shall I flee from thy presence?
If I ascend to heaven, thou art there!
   If I make my bed in Sheol, thou art there!
If I take the wings of the morning
   and dwell in the uttermost parts of the sea,
even there thy hand shall lead me,
   and thy right hand shall hold me.

My meditation ended with a remembrance of Don's lighting the Joy candle on the Advent wreath. The service ended, as per Don's instructions, with our standing together and singing "Joyful, Joyful, We Adore Thee."

The Postlude? "Joy to the World."

Take Care of My Daughter

The year before Don died and his home church embraced him, the saints of Compton Heights had already opened wide their arms for one of their own.

One of the blessings of my ministry has been the opportunity to serve with pastors making the transition from seminary and ordination into full-time ministry. Since 2007, I've worked with young pastors as a mentor for Bethany Fellows helping newly ordained, young pastors transition from seminary to sustained congregational ministry with a strong and healthy pastoral identity. When I was serving Compton Heights, I supervised three students from Eden Theological Seminary, a United Church of Christ seminary in nearby Webster Groves, MO. Donna Kendrick-Phillips, Cynthia Speller, and Jeanette Mott Oxford brought gifts and graces to Compton Heights that complemented (and supplemented!) my nascent gifts for ministry.

Supervision entailed our meeting for an hour in my office midweek and discussing specific instances of ministry they had been involved in. We'd plumb the incident for insights. *Why do you think you responded the way you did? What would you do differently? Did you sense the Spirit's presence? What biblical and theological themes were present?* Together, we would squint to perceive contours of grace, redemption, and healing, then seal the hour with prayer.

The year Jeanette was on staff, we were having a mid-year review during which we looked back over her first semester. She had offered her self-evaluation, and I was following up with my affirmation of her ministry with us, when she appeared to be on the verge of tears.

"Jeanette, is something wrong? I'm giving you a positive review. I hope that's clear."

"David," she said, "I need to tell you something. I'm a lesbian. I'm telling you because I came out to my ordination council and I'm now no longer a candidate for ordination."

She continued. "I was told I shouldn't have said anything. 'Don't ask. Don't tell.' But being a disciple of Jesus Christ calls us to be truthful, right? So, I told the truth. As a result, they voted to dismiss me."

Though in those years the United Church of Christ, Jeanette's home church, allowed for the ordination of LGBTQIA+ people at the national level – among the first to do so – it was left to the UCC's individual conferences, local bodies of churches, whether they would ordain or not. Jeanette's home conference in rural southern Illinois voted to not allow her to continue as a candidate for ordination. The reason, they told her, was they could not ordain a person no church would call as their pastor.

"You're a woman of such integrity," I said. "I admire you and I ache for you."

"David," she said, "There's one more thing. The *St. Louis*

Post-Dispatch got a hold of this and I've been told they may run it on the front page of Saturday's paper. I'm sorry for whatever may come of this when members of Compton read about it. I don't want to cause any problems for you or the congregation. You and they have been wonderful. I'll resign my position and leave quietly."

"Stop right there," I said. "You're not going anywhere. Let me call a few of the elders. I'll meet with them, tell them what happened, and get back to you with what they say."

With the publication of the front-page piece a few days off, time was of the essence. I called Walt and Cliff, two of Compton's elders, and asked them if they would come by the church at their earliest convenience. I needed their wisdom and counsel. They came that same afternoon. I told them what had transpired. My giving Jeanette a positive review of her first semester's ministry in our midst. Her tearing up. My asking her what was wrong. Her telling me she felt compelled to be truthful. The vote. The dismissal. The reason: no church would call her to be their pastor. I waited for their response.

We sat in the sanctuary in silence. What I remember is not that their prolonged silence kindled anxiety within me over what they would say. Rather, it signaled to me that I was in the presence of two men of prayer. Not prayer as in words spoken aloud, but prayer as leaning in humbly, respectfully, and expectantly to each other and to God. It was an exercise in corporate discernment, a mutual yielding, a bending of the knee of our hearts. A life was in the balance. A call to ministry. Jeanette had entrusted herself to us with courage, honesty, and sincerity.

I don't recall if Cliff or Walt spoke first. I do remember

what they proposed.

"David, tell Jeanette she has a church that welcomes her ministry. We want her here at Compton as our student pastor for the next semester."

Walt and Cliff then reached out to the other elders and gained their unanimous assent. To underscore their support, they directed me to invite Jeanette to teach a Sunday school class when the new semester began in January. She could choose the content. The elders would be her students along with anyone else who desired to attend.

Walt, Cliff, and I discussed the forthcoming newspaper article. Should we make an effort to give the congregation a heads up before Saturday? We ruled that out as not feasible. Jeanette would not be there on Sunday, having made plans weeks earlier to return to her home in southern Illinois to visit her father (Her mother had died the previous summer). I would make a statement during the announcements in worship to the effect, "You may have read in yesterday's *Post-Dispatch* a piece about our ministerial intern, Jeanette Oxford. Please know the elders and I have met, prayed together, and look forward to sharing our conversation with you after worship during today's Fellowship Supper." As I made the announcement, I saw nods of recognition on the faces of those who had read the piece as well as puzzled looks from those who had not.

One of the qualms I heard expressed during the lead up to the Fellowship Supper was, "I'm not sure how our older members will receive this."

After worship, as I made my way downstairs to Fellowship Hall, the first voice that greeted me was one of those older members. Ella, one of our senior saints, she who followed Jesus by clipping the toenails of nursing homes residents, was standing in the kitchen alongside Mary, servant of all God's children. Both were wearing aprons, serving spoons in hand.

"David," Ella asked in a loud voice, "Is *that* what all this about? Is *that* it? All morning I've been hearing whispers. I've seen people talking to each other in the hallway. Peep. Peep. Peep. Hush. Hush. Hush."

I deduced others had been talking among themselves about what they'd read in the paper and that Ella and Mary didn't have the least idea what had transpired. So as not to upset two of our senior members ("I'm not sure how our older members will receive this"), the news was being broadcast in clandestine cliques … in plain sight of two of our matriarchs.

The caution was unnecessary. In a voice loud enough for everyone within thirty feet to hear, aproned Ella, soup spoon in hand, Mary at attention alongside her, said, "Is all this hush hush about Jeanette being gay? Is that it? Is that all? You all had me worried! I thought something terrible had happened. For heaven's sake, we're all God's children, aren't we? Jeanette loves us and we love her. What's the problem? I wasn't born yesterday. Goodness gracious, I've known a lot of homosexuals in my lifetime. They're as good a people as you could ever know. There was a man that lived in the apartment building across the hall from where my husband and I lived in Columbia when we were first married – queer man – he was as nice as they come. You mean to tell me all this whispering this morning was about that? Love your neighbor. That's what Jesus said and that's what I say!"

With her righteous rant complete, Ella pirouetted from the sink to the stove, picked up a pot of soup, walked out of the kitchen into Fellowship Hall, set it down on the table, and barked, "Let's eat."

We did. The blessing had been said. It was time for communion … again.

When Jeanette got back, I shared with her the news of the weekend. Not the news printed on the front page of the *St. Louis Post Dispatch*, rather, the news proclaimed by the angels – Cliff, Walt, the elders, Ella and Mary – the good news proclaimed by the nods of Yes! and Of course! affirming her ministry spoken by those present in the basement of the church at table on the Lord's Day – the good news of God's all-embracing, all-inclusive love.

For that winter/spring semester, Jeanette taught, preached, and made pastoral visits at Compton. At their insistence, Jennie and I left our firstborn, two-year-old Will, with Jeanette and her partner Dorothy for many evenings of free babysitting. And at her year-end review in my office, she got another good review. Without tears. There was at least one church who would have her as their pastor.

With ordained ministry not an option, Jeanette took a position with Reform Organization of Welfare (ROWEL), a social justice advocacy organization. During those years, she became familiarized with Missouri's political landscape. In 2000, she filed and ran for a position as representative in the Missouri State legislature. She lost in the primary but found a position working for the American Lung Association advocating for healthcare for the poor. In 2004, she ran for office again and won, becoming the first openly lesbian legislator in the state. She was re-elected in 2006, 2008, and 2010. Term limits prevented her from seeking a fifth term in 2012.

When the article about her appeared on the front page of the *Post-Dispatch*, Jeanette knew word would reach her home community through its news outlets and word-of-mouth. She knew she needed to tell her father before he heard the news from another source. She told him she was sorry if what happened hurt his feelings or made him uncomfortable, but that she was doing the best she could to be an honest person and live as she felt called to live as a Christian.

With that, Jeanette says her father reached out, pulled her onto his lap, and prayed for her, saying, "This is all over my head, God. I don't understand any of this. But this is my little girl and you take care of her."

She said, "My dad didn't have a spot in his head that understood sexual orientation, but what he did understand was that I was his daughter and he loved me and he prayed for me. That's a really precious memory in my life." A precious memory, indeed. As is my memory of how Walt, Cliff, Ella, Mary, and congregation received Jeanette into the lap of grace and loved her.

I found Jeanette's address last year and sent her and Dorothy a Christmas card. I learned Jeanette now goes by the name of JMO (pronounced jay-mo) and uses the pronouns ze/zir/zirs.

I have friends and extended family members who grapple uncomfortably with gender fluidity, preferred pronouns, and so forth. To which all I can say is even if you don't feel comfortable with JMO's pronouns and can't get used to calling zir or someone you knew and loved by one name by a different name and pronouns, consider this: JMO's father didn't have a spot in his head that understood sexual orientation or preferred pronouns, but what he did understand was that ze was his daughter and he loved zir and prayed for zir.

These days, when people get up in arms about sexual orientation and its attendant dynamics, I remember Don lighting the Joy candle, Walt and Cliff's warmth and wisdom, and Ella in her apron asking, "Is *that* what all this is about? For heaven's sake, we're all God's children, aren't we?"

People can be so mean. Christians can be so cruel.

People can be so gracious. Christians can be so loving.

Be the latter.

God pulls the whole human family into the lap of grace and says, "Take care of my children."

That's what all this is about.

A Woman's Testimony

When the ordination council dropped Jeanette from candidacy, they named her sexual orientation as the stumbling block: no church would call her as their pastor. But back then and still today, just being a woman bars the door to ministry. The stone may have been rolled away from Jesus' tomb, but the refusal of some to allow the ancestors of the women who discovered the empty tomb to proclaim his resurrection remains firmly in place.

One Easter, our Five Church Association was invited to join other area churches in hosting an Easter Sunrise Service in Tower Grove Park. The Rev. Millie Slack and my colleague, the Rev. Peggy Harris, pastor of St. Luke's United Church of Christ, went to the planning meeting to represent FCA. They checked in with the secretary of the church hosting the meeting, who phoned upstairs to announce their arrival. Millie and Peggy found the meeting room and knocked on the door. The door opened a sliver, a voice inside said, "Hold on, please," then it was closed.

It stayed closed. Millie and Peggy stood in the hallway facing a closed door until they came to the sneaking suspicion they were not welcome. They had better things to do than wait in a church hallway facing a closed door, so they left. They could have walked in and caused a scene, but they were more polite than their so-called hosts, so they departed quietly.

The closed-door syndrome was due to their being "women ministers." When the men sequestered in that room heard from the secretary the sex of the clergy who had come to their planning meeting, they said, "Nothin' doin.'" I believe the official word communicated to Millie and Peggy was "Women may participate in the Easter Sunrise Service but may not stand behind the pulpit." There you have it: no preaching, no praying into a microphone, no reading Scripture from within the confines of a three-sided wooden podium unless you have a Y chromosome.

But God was not to be outdone that Easter. The risen Lord walked through closed doors and still does. It just so happened that as Peggy was driving back to St. Luke's, she turned into the parking lot of the Memorial Home, an assisted living center down the block from the church of the closed-door meeting. She parked her car and walked toward the door. In contrast to what she had just faced, the door was open.

Peggy made her way to the office and made a proposal. The churches of the Five Church Association would like to hold an Easter Sunrise Service on the lawn of the Memorial Home. Bring your wheelchairs, your walkers, your will to worship, and we'll have an Easter Sunrise Service right across the street from Tower Grove Park.

That is how it came to pass that fifty or so nursing home

residents and FCA members greeted Easter dawn together. And what do you know – some women participated in the service that glad morning. Sharon Clayton (a woman!) read the Easter story from behind a makeshift pulpit. She read the story right into the microphone loud and clear for all to hear. I heard her tell of the first witnesses to the resurrection – women! – who were told by the angel to "Go and tell" (read: "preach to") the other disciples that "He is Risen!" We closed by sharing together in the Lord's Supper. And guess who stood behind our makeshift Lord's Table and led us in the celebration? The Revs. Millie and Peggy – the two who had stood outside the stone-closed door.

The good ol' boys club was holding a service across the street somewhere in Tower Grove Park that morning. Fine. But the Church of the Risen Christ held a service that morning led by the descendants of "Mary Magdalene, Joanna, Mary the mother of James, and the other women" (Luke 24:9-10) who went out to the tomb that first Easter, found it empty, and were duly commissioned by the angel to go and tell everybody else. I was on the receiving end of their faithful testimony along with a passel of men and women astride their walkers and seated in their wheelchairs accompanied by their caregivers, men and women of many skin colors, a receptive congregation of all God's people.

The Scripture that Sharon Clayton read that Easter Sunrise Service was from Luke's Gospel. "Returning from the tomb, they told all this to the eleven and to all the rest. Now it was Mary Magdalene, Joanna, Mary the mother of James, and the other women with them who told this to the apostles" (24:9-10). Mark those words. Who did God entrust with the breaking news as press secretaries, spokespersons for the kingdom come, resurrection correspondents? Who were the first preachers of the Gospel? Women. We were just following God's lead on that first Easter Sunday: the first apostles (from the Greek word *apostello*, meaning sent) were women.

That first Easter, the gender of God's chosen messengers got in the way of God's message getting through to certain males. Luke tells us, "The women told this [news of the resurrection] to the apostles. But these words seemed to them an idle tale and they did not believe them" (Luke 24:11). The women's story seemed like "an idle tale" to the men. Other translations read "empty talk," "a silly story," "a foolish yarn," "utter nonsense," "sheer humbug." This is the only occurrence of the Greek word λῆρος (lēros) in the New Testament. I wonder if our word *leery* is related to it. To think that the women raced home from the tomb, banged on the door of the disciples, and told them what had happened only to have those men guffaw, pshaw, and go back to bed, muttering, "I know what they said, but I'm leery. Resurrection? C'mon! Just a bunch of women preachers."

Let me add this interesting detail: in those days, a woman's testimony was inadmissible in a court of law. No woman could be called as a witness. The *Mishnah*, the record of Jewish law that was written down around 200 CE reads, "From women let not evidence be accepted because of the levity and temerity of their sex." Levity: silliness. Temerity: recklessness. A woman's testimony was not deemed credible.

I can still hear my grandfather, Gabe Shirey, when my grandmother, Mamie Mae, got to talking about something. She'd get more and more animated until he'd roll his eyes and blurt out his best (worst) hen imitation, "Cluck, cluck, cluck, cluck, cluck!" I imagine him having breakfast with Peter, James, John and the boys. There's a knock on the door. He overhears some women excitedly tell about a stone rolled away, an empty tomb, and men in dazzling apparel, saying, "He's not here, He's risen!" He rolls his eyes and clucks.

Do you believe a woman's testimony? Today we have the #MeToo movement accompanied by allegations leveled against men in high places: celebrities, sports figures, and politicians. Is a woman's testimony to be believed? The court of law in Jesus' day ruled women's testimony inadmissible. Grandpa Shirey ruled it unacceptable. The first apostles were *leery*. Millie and Peggy faced a closed door. Can anybody of any gender, make, model, or sexual orientation who is open to God's leading be used by God as a messenger of God's truth and grace? Nonsense or Godsense?

We can each come up with a list of ministers who are blessed to our memories. I give thanks for sisters in Christ across my ministry who, in the face of closed doors, ears, and hearts, proclaim the gospel. I was preceded at Compton by the Rev. Arla Elston. During the formative years of my ministry in St. Louis, Millie, Peggy and the Rev. Margie Pride, colleague at Memorial Boulevard Christian Church in St. Louis, modelled what a ministry of justice, mercy, and humility looks like. The Rev. Dr. Jacque Foster was called to Compton seven years after I left and served faithfully for over twenty-five years.

If we're all created in the image of God, then all of us are innately, inherently able to bear witness to God. That includes preaching, pastoring, and teaching. There were and still are folks who would bar the door to ministry to those who are lacking a Y chromosome, but that's nonsense to me. My life and ministry have been informed, enlightened, challenged, liberated, blessed, and enriched by the descendants of Miriam, Deborah, Priscilla, Phoebe, Junia, and the Marys, women for whom sealed tombs and closed doors are not able to bury their gifts or mute their voices.

Love In Any Language

Marie was a resident at the Memorial Home where we had our Easter sunrise service. She and her husband, Paul Sr., were longtime Compton Heights members. Their son, Paul Jr., his wife, Sue, and their children Tammy, Vaughn, and Cheryl, were active members as well. I had the pleasure of marrying Tammy as well as Cheryl and dedicating Tammy's first child. Three generations of the same family to pastor. All were a pleasure.

When Paul Sr. died, part of Marie's soul went with him. Not long after, Marie had a stroke – tongue, mouth, and mind could no longer work together to produce the words that produce the sentences that give voice to thoughts. To "speak" with Marie I had to get the chart from her chest of drawers that had the alphabet printed on it. Marie pointed to each letter and spelled out each word, piecing together her thoughts letter by letter and word by word.

Atop her chest of drawers was a picture of Marie and Paul. Marie wore a broad grin in the photo. She stood tall in a lovely yellow satin evening dress. Her hair was done up just right. She wore a corsage of red roses. Next to Marie was her husband. Paul wore a broad grin that rivaled Marie's. He stood tall, too, in a dapper outfit that complemented his wife's. He sported a floppy yellow satin bow tie that matched Marie's dress. Before the happy couple was a festively decorated cake – white frosting, red trim, a nifty double-decker. A glad occasion – perhaps a fiftieth wedding anniversary. The picture was a reminder of happier days.

Despite her stroke, Marie could still communicate. She could still get across what she was thinking and feeling. One Sunday, after conducting chapel services at The Memorial Home, I visited her, taking Jennie and our infant son Will with me. At first, I dominated the "conversation." I held her hand, told her who I was, sat our son Will on her bed and put his tiny wriggling hand in hers. Marie's eyes smiled.

Then it was Marie's turn. I held the alphabet chart in front of her. She pointed to letters and began to spell – P-R-X-V-E-Q-I. Oops, I thought, we're not getting anywhere. We started over, but with the same scrambled result.

Marie was obviously frustrated. She was trying to tell us something before we left. Another try. More scrambled letters. But just as I was about to go, Marie reached out and grabbed my hand. Slowly, but with great determination, she pulled my hand toward her, right up to her face, closed her eyes, and gently kissed it.

Her eyes then opened and she looked up at me as if to say, "Now do you understand?"

I did. Love in any language communicates clearly. Deep within each of us is the need to love and be loved. Will and Marie, though at opposite ends of life's journey, possessed that heartfelt need. Though neither of them could spell out letter, word, and sentence and both appeared sometimes as babbling meaninglessly, they each were driven by the purest of all desires – to love and be loved.

It has taken me over five hundred words correctly spelled out and pieced together to express this truth, but all Marie had to do was grasp my hand and lead it to her lips. Which of us was most able to express ourselves most effectively? And, in that room in The Memorial Home that Sunday, who ministered to whom?

The Laughing Man

When Jennie and I pulled the Ryder truck up to the back door of our apartment in the two-family flat on Utah Place south of Tower Grove Park, one of the things I looked forward to most was setting up my very own study. After having gone through four years of seminary when the kitchen table had to do double duty as a desk, when my Bible, typewriter, and commentaries shared space with a toaster and salt and pepper shakers, visions of a room reserved for a desk and bookshelves arose frequently. So it was that on the first day Jennie and I set foot in the apartment, I earmarked the 10' x 12' room at the end of the front hallway as my study.

It had a short lifespan. A few months after we moved in, Jennie began referring to my room at the end of the hallway as the nursery. At first, I resisted, insisting the room be referred to as my study until February. But there came a day when, as I sat at my desk, typewriter before me, books within arm's reach, there was a crib to my left where my files once were. Colorful clowns with red balloons set against a red checkered background looked out at me from behind the bars of the crib. Neatly stacked in the crib were gifts for our child, many hand-made, all of them thoughtfully chosen. There were knitted blankets, quilts, receiving blankets, washcloths, bibs, shirts, onesies, and hooded towels. Under the crib, a highchair was laid next to a baby carrier and next to them, side-by-side, diapers and a potty chair. Behind me was a changing table whose underneath compartments were stocked with rattles, booties, powders, creams, more diapers, and ducky diaper pins. All those visible expressions of the church's love surrounded me as I sat at my desk.

There was a picture that hung above my desk that has never ceased to delight me. It is a photograph titled "Laughing Man," a black and white photo of a man who is roaring with laughter. His eyes are drawn closed – he is on the verge of tears. His mouth is open in a wide toothless grin. Everything about him exudes laughter. As I looked up at him while at my desk one evening with Jennie's due date drawing near, I couldn't help but to chuckle myself. The old rascal was laughing at me as he looked out over my shoulder at smiling clowns, teddy bears, bright balloons, booties, and ducky diaper pins. *Some pastor's study, buddy!* He was laughing out loud at me, and I couldn't help but to laugh with him.

It was all starting to sink in. In a few weeks, I'd be a father. My child would rest comfortably among the gifts of a congregation's love in the room at the end of the hallway – the nursery. I'd be relegated to the kitchen table with my typewriter and books, the salt and pepper shakers and the toaster, The Laughing Man mocking me from his perch.

When I began at Compton Heights, I learned that one of my responsibilities was to write a weekly newsletter column. My first efforts at writing anything other than a paper for class or a sermon for Sunday originated in what was my study. When Will was born and I was evicted, I wrote my columns at a workspace Jennie set up for me in what doubled as a dining room. Printed on the front and back of a sheet of colored legal paper (one week green, one week pink, the next week marigold, the next week yellow), my secretary, June, would type my column along with the week's news onto a stencil, cut out a few doodles to accompany the posts (it wasn't called clip art for nothing), and glue them to the stencil. She'd then fire up the mimeograph machine and churn out (thrum, thrum, thrum) one hundred fifty copies of the *Compton Heights Christian*, its masthead a hand drawn sketch of an urban skyline with a steeple in its midst. I can smell the inky fragrance of our makeshift printing press to this day.

Those first newsletters at Compton Heights began with what was titled A WORD FROM DAVID. Catchy title, huh? My column was due first thing every Monday morning. Every Sunday, a sermon; every Monday, a newsletter article. When I balked one day to June about being on a deadline two days in a row, delivering a sermon on Sunday (Jennie's dad used to say, "Sunday comes around with embarrassing regularity") and then turning in a newsletter column on Monday, she said, "How about not doing it? Do you really think people read these?" Rather than receiving her retort as permission to not write, I received it as a challenge. "I don't know if these are read or not," I said, "but I'm going to try to offer something worthwhile."

There began forty years of writing newsletter columns, a practice I never begrudged. Across the years, as technology developed, mimeograph machines gave way to the first generation of computers. I'd type my column onto a PC, save it to a floppy disk the size of a 45 record, and hand it to my secretary. The final product would then be duplicated on an unreliable copier, a process interrupted by paper jams, the cleaning of rollers, and allowing the machine to cool down. We knew the Xerox service technician on a first name basis. In time, everything was done digitally. I'd type my column, save it as a Word or . pdf document, and send it to Clay, our Communications Coordinator, as an attachment. He would then format it for e-mailing at 1 p.m. on Wednesday and post it on the Facebook page.

My first order of business upon retiring was to set up a place in which to do business, whatever that business would turn out to be. Though its contours were blurry (but I'd figure it out), I knew that business would include writing. My mentor and friend Don Schutt is wont to ask, "What makes your heart sing?" For the forty years of my ministry, rarely a day went by that I did not write something – a newsletter column, sermon, blog post, letter, email, Bible study, or my morning journal entry. The time I spent writing, though work, wasn't work at all. It was a pleasure.

I told my friend Gary, also a retired pastor who continues to write, "I can't not write." After fifty years of running, I'm addicted to "the runner's high" that follows miles of physical exertion, pickin' 'em up and puttin' 'em down. I'm convinced there's also some sort of endorphin-charged release that is the fruit of picking out words and putting them down for as long as it takes to make meaning or sense of something, tell a story, or record something I heard or saw that delighted me.

If only for the personal gratification that accompanies putting slivers of my life into words for safekeeping and future savoring – the composition of a verbal scrapbook – I'm going to continue to write.

Where? For most of my ministry, I did my writing in my study at the church. I harbored the hope I'd have a study at home, but Will was followed by two sisters who occupied the additional rooms Jennie and I acquired in the homes we lived in during their growing-up years. There was no room for my study during our children's growing up years.

When at long last we were empty nesters, the freed-up rooms became guest bedrooms, not conducive for a study, and during the last eight years of my ministry, though our home had an extra room on the second floor that I claimed as my future study from the get-go, Jennie did such a good job of transforming the church's Senior Minister's office into hospitable space that I put down my writing roots there and left the room upstairs at home unaddressed. It bided its time until I retired.

So it was that the one-time father of a newborn son who gave up his study for the raising of a family was a retired grandfather who had a fourth bedroom – space Jennie says was probably a nursery at some point – to turn into a writing den.

The late Frederick Buechner is one of my "paper mentors," someone whose writing has blessed my ministry and tutored my way of living. His iconic words, "Listen to your life. See it for the fathomless mystery that it is," have fanned the flames of my desire to mine the unfolding of my own life to write perceptively, honestly, and well. As I reread his memoirs during COVID, a lifeline to beauty, sanity, and holiness during that ugly travail, I was reminded of his beloved study/library/sitting room at his homestead in rural Vermont, a room he dubbed the Magic Kingdom. As I read the verbal tour he gives the reader of that space made sacred to him by photos, books, trinkets, and mementos, I experienced the anticipatory delight of becoming the architect/designer of my own consecrated space.

So it was that in the first weeks of my retirement, Jennie came to my side. She did what she does best – what makes *her* heart sing – which is to bring order out of chaos a la God churning creation cream out of the disorderly Deep (Genesis 1:2). She turned the room upstairs into my study. My desk is next to a window that looks out on a magnificent maple tree. People pull over in the fall and take pictures of its blazing canopy of orange leaves. I write in its shade. Hence, I've dubbed my writer's den The Maple Loft. Gifted to me by Jennie's gifts for order, décor, and beauty, I'm spending this chapter of my life savoring the gifts accrued over forty years of ministry listening to others' lives, glimpsing in them the fathomless mystery they are, and writing about it. In anticipation of the pondering, praying, and writing that will unfold here in The Maple Loft, the endorphins are doing their work deep down within where quiet joy and words are born.

As for the Laughing Man who mocked me forty years ago from my study that became my firstborn's nursery, he's now hanging above my dresser in the bedroom. I'm not sure what he's laughing at these days and I'm not going to ask. I'm happy to have a place to write at long last, including writing books like this one in which many of the stories I wrote over forty years of ministry that were turned in as newsletter columns can find their place alongside each other in the longer narrative a book affords.

I hear June ask, "Do you really think people read them?"

To which I say, "Absolutely! People read my books. I've sold dozens worldwide!"

And the Laughing Man laughs.

Roach Wrath

The Laughing Man would have gotten a kick out of the shenanigans that kept me laughing at Compton, including the Sunday of the roach race.

Back in 1984, singer-songwriter Ray Stevens released a hilarious song about a squirrel that wandered into a worship service at the First Self-Righteous Church in Pascagoula, Mississippi, causing an uproar among the faithful. It's a catchy tune with wacky lyrics, the chorus of which went,

> *The day the squirrel went berserk*
> *In the First Self-Righteous Church*
> *In that sleepy little town of Pascagoula*
> *It was a fight for survival that broke out in revival*
> *They were jumpin' pews and shouting "Hallelujah!"*

Silly? Sure. Corny? Yes. Unbelievable? Well, yes, but an equally uproarious song could have been written about the goings-on in Compton's sanctuary one Sunday.

I prepared that Sunday's sermon with much trepidation. After all, I was wrestling with a thorny issue, namely, the wrath of God. Having never preached on fire and brimstone, I crafted my sermon with special care. After having everything in place and entitling the message "The Merciful Wrath of God," I was all set to go when Sunday morning came around.

After the Scripture was read, I stepped into the pulpit and launched into my frightful theme. As I recall, I got off to a pretty good start. I was just getting into a vivid description of the wrath of God as depicted in Psalm 18 complete with smoke coming out of God's nostrils and fire leaping forth from God's mouth when I was aware of a commotion in the soprano section of the choir to my right. One of our sopranos was laughing.

I was puzzled, to say the least. I was in the midst of a soliloquy on the wrath of God and one of my choir members was tittering. I tried to make sense of it but could not. I thought there might be a gaping hole in the seat of my trousers, but I had my robe on. I then surmised someone had whispered a joke that evoked the guffaw. The snickering rippled outward from the initiating soprano to the rest of the soprano section and into the altos. Harmonized hilarity. But why?

I was no stranger to muffled laughter in the choir. I had been a contributor to such the previous December, my first at Compton, during the annual Christmas cantata. During one of the rehearsals, as the handful of us who sang the bass, baritone, and tenor parts were singing the story of the wise men, one of us got to laughing. My remembrance is that it was induced by our recognizing the over-the-top schlock we were singing straight-faced accompanied by a saccharine sweet, overdone melody. To this day I can remember the lyric and melody: *We are the wise men who've come from afar / Camelback, onward, we follow the star.*

I don't remember who did it, but during one of the umpteen times we rehearsed that line, one of the men dramatically raised his hand in a salute-like gesture above his brow, then turned his head back and forth from side to side in slow motion as if earnestly looking into the distance for yonder star. The gesture and dramatic flair that accompanied it was as over-the-top as the lyric and music. Tired after a full day, we were slaphappy. It got us tickled. There went the rehearsal. Just the sound of the notes that led into the wise men melody evoked our laughter, muted our singing, and required our starting over. Adding to the frivolity was the cluelessness of Lynwood, our choir director, who, in Absent-Minded Professor fashion, never seemed to notice either our cracking up when we reached the kings' chorale or our raised hands above our brows gesture when we sang it.

On the Sunday morning when we presented the cantata and the measures drew near for our men's section entrance, it was all I could do not to raise my hand. Nor did I dare make eye contact with the other men, especially Cliff in the tenor section or his son Darrell sandwiched between him and me, both of whom were in on the joke and both of whom were, in my peripheral vision, looking straight ahead trying to sing while stifling guffaws. I've remained in touch with Darrell over nearly forty years now, and part of our getting back together and reminiscing about days gone by calls for one of us to raise the hand and commence the singing, *"We are the wise men...."* No laughter is better than laughter that refuses to be shushed into staid silence in a sanctuary. With that history, I had no right to begrudge whatever was happening in the choir the day my wrath sermon went awry.

I was baffled. Cliff and Darrell showing no indication of being party to what was happening. The congregation seemed to be unaware of the chancel chuckles, so I continued my sermon, expostulating next on the Day of Judgement. A paragraph or so into that warning of gloom and doom, another soprano got into the act. Rather than laughing, though, she had an anguished look on her face. Her eyes were open wide, and her mouth was agape. At first, I thought she was responding to my rhetorical eloquence, caught up in the horrors of Judgement Day as proclaimed by the prophet Malachi (4:1-3), Jesus (Luke 21:25-28), and her twenty-seven-year-old pastor. She was paying no attention to me, however. She was looking in the direction of the communion table at some unidentified object that by this time had attracted the attention of yet another soprano, an alto or two, and Jim Clayton in the corner of the bass section two pews back.

Now I was really puzzled. What was going on back there? By this time, I was well into a vigorous condemnation of all that is evil, but my choir was oblivious to my preaching. They were transfixed by the underside of the communion table. For a moment, I was tempted to step out of the pulpit and continue my sermon from behind the communion table so I could take a peek at what had caught their attention, but I determined to follow through to the end. At least the rest of the congregation hadn't been distracted yet.

So it was that I forged ahead through judgement and wrath to promised mercy. I wrapped it up in a paragraph or two, said Amen, and returned to my seat behind the pulpit, casting a stink eye at the choir on the way. The evocations of tittering and terror remained.

After the service was over, a repentant soprano filled me in on the reason for the commotion. When I heard her explanation, I nodded my head in disbelief and then broke out in laughter in concert with her renewed chuckles and the cackling of a few other choir members who were in the know.

Evidently, a certain multilegged creature belonging to Kingdom Animalia, Phylum Arthropoda, Class Insecta and Order Blattaria – aka, a cockroach – made an appearance on the communion table, ran a few laps, descended one leg of the Lord's Table to the floor of the chancel, and skedaddled toward the choir. The little rascal then spent the duration of my sermon scurrying around the vicinity of the soprano section leaving in its wake a host of reactions ranging from muffled laughter to muted screams. The little bugger even scaled the modesty rail and shook its antennae at one of our altos before dashing off toward unknown territory. All of this transpired as I was trying to engage in a serious exposition of the wrath of God.

The next Sunday, I vowed to take a peek under the communion table and in the general vicinity of the choir before worship began just in case that reprobate insect got any ideas. And I was tempted to write Ray Stevens a note and tell him his tale about the squirrel getting loose in a church service was all right, but I had an even better story to offer for his next song.

Better yet, maybe he could write a Christmas cantata.

Wrestling with God

When Darrell, my star-seeking wise man compatriot, wasn't standing next to me in the choir, he and his soprano section wife, Marty, were engaged in a more serious quest for spiritual enrichment uninterrupted by rogue insects. As I was learning to pray in the months following my dad's death, I asked others who evidenced a vital spirituality if they would like to get together over a meal and talk about matters of faith and life. The Shalom Group was born. We met in Chris and Bonnie's apartment on the second floor of a two-family flat on Arsenal St. overlooking Tower Grove Park. Darrell and Marty, Cliff and Edna, Bonnie's sister Becky, Will and Anne, Mary, and Sallie joined us. A baker's dozen.

Christianity is a team sport. Most of the times the pronoun you appears in the Bible it is first person plural. We mistakenly read that you as first-person singular, individualize the message, and miss the context: the Bible is addressed to a community of people seeking to do life together. Growth in faith occurs when you're linked to like-minded others who will encourage and hold you accountable for doing the things disciples of Jesus do.

Beginning with the Shalom Group and continuing in all my places of ministry, I sought out others whose companionship in Christ would help me grow. In North Carolina, it was Mike during lunch hour runs from the YMCA followed by lunch at the Goody Goody Omelet House. I also had the Monday Lunch Bunch with Baptist, Lutheran, Presbyterian, and Adventist pastors at the First Baptist Church Activities Center and The Fellowship of the Carpenters, a men's group, who met in my office Wednesday mornings at 7:30 a.m. In Columbus, IN, I met weekly with three local pastors for breakfast in the dining room of the hospital. In Arizona, my spirit was sustained by a Thursday morning breakfast at The Good Egg with a quartet of pastors. In Lexington, I was invited into an interracial, ecumenical lectionary Bible Study that met in the upstairs library of Good Shepherd Episcopal Church. When COVID struck, we met by Zoom and continue to do so. Though some members of our group have been called to other churches in other cities, we convene on Wednesday mornings at 9:30 am around the lectionary passages for the week. Every Saturday morning at 9:30 am, I talk for an hour with Matt, the best man at my wedding. We go deep. Don, Kim, Gary, and Bob, colleagues and mentors from Bethany Fellows, have been prayer partners for seventeen years and counting. We say we do life together.

If I could suggest one practice capable of deepening the life of faith, it would be to ponder Acts 2:42: "And they (plural!) devoted themselves to the apostles teaching and fellowship, to the breaking of the bread and the prayers." Then ask, "How can I translate the practices of this sentence concretely and specifically into my life?" and "Who can I ask to do it with me?"

In addition to gathering at his apartment for the Shalom Group on Sunday evenings, Chris and I met many a Monday night to quench our thirst and talk over matters of faith. With the Anheuser Busch Brewery sending plumes of malted hops wafting over the city, St. Louis has pubs dotting the corners of many a southside neighborhood. After a Monday night meeting, Chris and I would walk a mile from the church to our chosen venue a few blocks from where we lived called Blackthorn Pub. We learned from the proprietor that before he bought the place it was notorious for fights and rough-housing. When he bought the bar, the first thing he did was play classical music on the jukebox. It flushed out the rowdies in no time.

I learned during our years in the Shalom Group that what classical music did to brawling bikers, the call to deepening devotion can do to some Christians – cause them to head for the doors. One Sunday night, as we wrestled with something that was stretching us beyond where we were to where we sensed God was calling us to be, Sallie said, "I'll be honest. I only want to go so far with my religion."

Jesus was transparent in delineating the demands of discipleship, saying, "Pick up your cross and come follow" (Matthew 16:24). In turn, many would-be disciples have been just as transparent in protesting the more exacting responsibilities of discipleship. Of the cross, Peter said, "God forbid it, Lord!" (Matthew 16:22). Of whatever it was the Shalom Group was considering that Sunday night, Sallie demurred. She and we only want to go so far with our religion.

A bumper sticker I saw once read "If you love Jesus, tithe.

Any fool can honk." The same challenge holds for other requisite acts to which Christians are called: loving our enemies, doing justice, and forgiving seven times seventy times come to mind. List your own dictums of Jesus you wish he hadn't said. Truth be told, we're happy to let Jesus bear the cross while we stand back at a safe, comfortable distance. We only want to go so far with our religion.

We need people alongside us who will challenge us to go further. One of my seminary professors, Don Beisswenger, was one of those people. Don was taken by the story found in Genesis 32 of Jacob's long night on the banks of the Jabbok River. Alone, he wrestled until sunrise with a man? an angel? God? The text is mysteriously vague. He called the name of the place Penuel. Don opened a retreat center north of Nashville in the Tennessee hills called Penuel Ridge. I thought to myself, "Call it Peaceful Pastures or Mountain's Majesty or Blessed Breezes or even Happy Holler. But Penuel Ridge? Who wants to wrestle with God?" I was remembering Sallie's honest admission: "I only want to go so far with my religion."

Like it or not, though, we all may have to go to Penuel. We may not have a choice when it comes to wrestling with God. I received a geography lesson in studying the Penuel passage. The Jabbok River where the wrestling took place flowed between Jacob and the Promised Land. My conclusion based on that geography lesson is this: everyone on a genuine journey of faith must pass through the Jabbok and spend a night, a week, a month, even years at Penuel wrestling with God. I'm convinced every genuine journey of faith requires passing through Penuel and wrestling with God.

There is a chorus you may be familiar with that has a

kick to it: "Spirit of the living God, fall afresh on me. Melt me, mold me, fill me, use me." That verse suggests that before God can fill us and use us, God must first melt us and mold us. Do you realize what is involved in a body's being melted and molded? We're not talking about a relaxing massage here. We're talking about a full-scale reconstruction project, an arduous tearing down and rebuilding of the way we think, act, and talk. Before God can really use us, we must first be melted and molded. We must wrestle with God.

Geography and theology both say we must go to Penuel to get to the Promised Land.

There are times in our lives that take us to that place of wrestling with God. What are some of them? Grappling with important decisions. Striving to discern God's will. Breaking through to deeper commitments to God and one another. Pressing beyond our comfort zones, putting ourselves in places and situations that will stretch and challenge us. Struggling to free ourselves from destructive habits, attitudes, and actions; grappling with addictions that hold us captive. There's no wrestling like repenting of wrongs, forgiving, and being forgiven. Max Lucado describes such moments as "anvil time." We're being hammered out, reshaped, reformed. When we're on the anvil, we're at Penuel.

Which raises a question. If we all must go there, what becomes of wrestlers with God? In the Bible story, Jacob walked off with a limp. It's true. Anyone who dares enter deeply into life with God or any other person, pouring out body, mind, soul, and might, will walk with a limp. Anyone who has raised children or grandchildren walks with a limp. Anyone who has shared life with another human being in the bonds of marriage, partnership, or close friendship walks with a limp. Anyone who has invested themselves in the life of a congregation, from the worship services to the meetings, walks with a limp. Anyone who earnestly tries to follow Jesus in their dealings with everybody everywhere walks with a limp.

But mind you, there was a blessing at Penuel. God blessed Jacob at the end of the night of wrestling. As the sun rose, Jacob walked off with a new name, a changed man. His new name was Israel, meaning "wrestles with God." Which says to me that to be one of God's chosen is by definition to be a person who wrestles with God. It's a strange paradox to be sure. Wrestling, though it leaves one with a limp, is a blessing nonetheless. But it's true: to contend with God is the greatest adventure and joy of all. Life with God and growth in faith at its invigorating best takes place not in the comfy confines of Jerusalem but in the scratch and scrawl of Penuel, wrestling with God.

When I was a kid, my brother, sister, and I would sneak up on my dad as he lay on the family room floor watching television. We'd pounce on him at a predetermined signal – me at his strong right arm, my brother, Mike, at his left, my sister, Jill, lunging to wrap herself around his legs – hoping to wrestle him to the point of surrender. If we all did our part to immobilize him, one of us could reach out with a free hand and tickle him under his neck, a move that would cause him to convulse in laughter. It was great fun! But he'd inevitably wriggle free. Then he'd get one of us in the infamous leg-lock and another in the notorious arm-vise. The third of us would be pulled against his chin and get the dreaded bear rub, his whiskers rubbing up against our cheeks like sandpaper until we'd call out, "Let go! Stop! Mom, tell him to let go! Dad, stop! You're hurting me! Meany!" And he'd let go and we'd walk off, red-faced, sweating, hair matted, gasping for breath.

"That'll teach you to wrestle with me!" he'd say triumphantly as we limped toward the kitchen. Five minutes later, we'd head back for more.

The lunging, the laughing, the sweating, the grunting, even the crying and limping off utterly defeated – what a blessing that wrestling was! Dad's been dead 37 years now. What I'd give for another night of wrestling with him.

The Scripture says of Jacob renamed Israel, "The sun rose upon him as he passed Penuel, limping because of his thigh." What a blessing it is to wrestle with God! I learned that precious truth in an upper room apartment on Arsenal Street across from Tower Grove Park alongside Darrell and Marty, Cliff and Edna, Will and Anne, Chris, Bonnie, Becky, Mary, Jennie ... and Sallie. We called ourselves the Shalom Group. Together, we wrestled with God.

Tribute

One of the benefits of keeping a journal as I have for nearly forty years is the sacrament of etching onto paper the people, places, and experiences sacred to me, creating a verbal scrapbook. Many of these stories were originally scribbled into my journal, some of them to be submitted to June on a Monday morning as a newsletter column or preserved across four decades to be included in this book. My friend and mentor, Gary, says he prays at the point of a pen. His daily journal is his prayer book, its entries psalms of petition, remembrance, and thanksgiving.

In 1987, while in my second year at Compton Heights, Jennie and I attended our church's biennial international assembly in Louisville, KY. On Sunday, we drove from Louisville to the historic Cane Ridge Meeting House in Bourbon County, one of the birthplaces of our Disciples of Christ denomination. After the program at Cane Ridge, friends asked if we'd like to join them for worship in nearby Paris, KY, at Seventh Street Christian Church, one of our historic African American congregations.

"Meet you there," we said.

We were greeted at the door by a genial, dignified man who introduced himself as Elder Reed. When we told him we were ministers and spouses attending the Disciples of Christ assembly in Louisville, he exclaimed, "The Lord is surely at work this morning! A member of our pastor's extended family is having a medical emergency and he just left for the hospital. The Lord sent you pastors to lead us in worship. One of you is going to pray, one is going to preside at the Lord's table, and one of you is going to preach."

Before I could get a word in edgewise, one of my colleagues said, "I'll take the prayer." The other quickly volunteered, "I'll serve at the table." At which time Elder Reed looked at me and said, "You're our preacher." He reached out and shook my trembling hand as my colleagues chuckled under their breath.

I preached. Somehow. I came up with a thought and expounded on it extemporaneously, carried along by the verbal encouragement of the congregation. A Hammond organ's swelling chords undergirded my crescendo to the finish. I returned to my seat with a side glance to my colleagues.

After the Benediction, Elder Reed asked me to stand at the door and greet the congregation. They were graciously complimentary. He was last in line.

Ten days later, I received a letter at our apartment in St. Louis. It had a Paris, Kentucky, postmark and the return address of William B. Reed. It read:

Dear Rev. Shirey,
We definitely are considering changing pastors by the beginning of the fiscal year 1988. Would you ever con-

sider the pastoring of an all black church? I have contacted the membership about you and the response was encouraging. Would you, if interested, please send full particulars as to salary, etc. I believe should you accept you will never have cause to regret your decision.

Sincerely,
William B. Reed – Elder

I wrote a letter thanking Elder Reed for the honor of being deemed worthy of consideration but having only been in my position at Compton Heights for two years, I couldn't consider a new call. I reiterated my gratitude for his welcome and the encouragement of my nascent ministry his letter represented. I have kept it to this day.

After I was called to serve Central Christian Church in Lexington, KY, in 2014, I googled *William B. Reed, Paris, KY,* and found an entry in the database of Notable Kentucky African Americans:

Reed, William B. "Chief" (born: 1912 - died: 1996) William B. Reed, born in Paris, KY, was the last principal of the segregated Western School for Negroes. The Paris City Schools were fully integrated in 1966. Reed would become the first African American Assistant Principal in the Paris City School system. He was also the first to become a city commissioner in Paris. Reed had been a star football and basketball player at Kentucky State College [now Kentucky State University] and coached the Western High basketball team to a national championship in 1953. He was also the school's football coach. Reed was the first African American elected to the Paris City Council in 1977. The William "Chief" Reed Park in Paris is named in his honor.

I decided a field trip was in order. I followed my GPS on a fifty-mile round trip from Lexington to Chief Reed Park in Paris to pay my respects. What I found both warmed and troubled me. The park dedicated to the acclaimed athlete, coach, teacher, mentor, public servant, civil rights pioneer, and churchman is out of the way in a low-income neighborhood. Just before the park is an unwelcoming NO OUTLET sign; just beyond it is the city dump.

I parked and got out, the only person there on a gray, wintry Sunday morning, and walked over to a plaque honoring Mr. Reed's legacy. The dump, the NO OUTLET sign, an esteemed man's enduring legacy etched onto bronze for the ages – there's a sermon there somewhere, but that's for another day.

Today I sit in wonder at the reception my colleagues and I received at the welcoming right hand of Elder Reed at Seventh Street Church in 1987 juxtaposed with the reception his ancestors received at Cane Ridge nearly two hundred years earlier. Black congregants were relegated to the balcony of the Meeting House, accessible not by stairs from within the sanctuary but by climbing ladders propped against the outside of the building and crawling through second story windows.

The last words Elder Reed wrote in his letter inviting me to consider serving as pastor of Seventh Street remain with me to this day: "I believe should you accept you will never have cause to regret your decision." I have no regrets about the way my ministry unfolded across the decades. It would have been inappropriate for me to leave Compton Heights after only two years, a church whose people, ministry, and mission left an indelibly positive mark on me. But whenever I glimpse Elder Reed's letter out of the corner of my eye, I wonder *What if?*

The Sunday I made my pilgrimage to Chief Reed Park to pay homage, after I reached out and touched the bronze plaque with his visage and dates etched on it, church bells began tolling in the distance, adding a sacred soundtrack to my vigil. I returned to my car and drove back to Lexington. Sitting at my desk, I reread his letter, then folded it and returned it to its well-worn #10 business envelope. Reminded again of the enduring benediction that is his affirmation of my ministry thirty-seven years ago, a draft chapter dedicated to his memory complete, I closed my notebook, his name enshrined within, black ink on white pages.

Touch the Plaque

The year after I was introduced to Elder Reed, I led a couple dozen of our Compton Heights members on what was billed as a Disciples Heritage trip to Cane Ridge. The birthplace of our movement, Cane Ridge was the site of a revival in 1801 at which a pastor by the name of Barton Warren Stone experienced a powerful movement of God's Spirit that changed his life. He eventually moved to Lexington and in 1816 founded what is today Central Christian Church (Disciples of Christ) where I was privileged to serve as Senior Minister from 2014 until my retirement in 2022. Though it is only at an elevation of 843 feet, Cane Ridge was a mountaintop experience for Barton W. Stone.

We worshipped in the venerable Meeting House. Jennie played the old pump organ. I dressed up like Barton W. Stone in a black frock coat with tails and preached. After the service, I noticed a bronze plaque on the way out that reads:

> *The West Door of Cane Ridge Meeting House*
> *is dedicated to Missionaries*
> *who have responded to the call*

to proclaim the Word of God
to all people everywhere

I looked at my first flock of disciples mingling after worship and saw them in all their precious uniqueness. Darrell and Marty. Cliff and Edna. Virgil and Mary. Pauline. Jean. Carol and her mother Lillian. Dorothy. Don. Jeanette. Mary. Ethel. Jim and Sharon. Juana and her daughters, Wanda and Patty. Young and old. Black and white. There I was at twenty-seven years old dressed up like a preacher, but underneath the costume so raw, so green. Yet there we were, the spiritual heirs of those who went out the west door of Cane Ridge nearly two hundred years earlier, themselves heirs of those who had gone down the west side of a Galilean mountain nearly 1,800 years before that. Not knowing what else to do, I whispered a prayer, reached out and touched the bronze plaque, and headed west with my flock of St. Louisans to be disciples of Jesus Christ.

In 1995, seven years later, I brought a bus load from our church in North Carolina to Cane Ridge. Again upon leaving, I touched the bronze plaque, after which we got in the bus to be driven west to Lexington where we were given a tour of historic Central Christian Church. Little did I know it at the time that I'd be called to Central twenty years later.

In 2003, I was flown from Phoenix, where Jennie and I were planting a new church from scratch amid sagebrush and saguaro cactus, to Lexington, to attend a training event with new church planters from across the country. We caravaned to Cane Ridge for a worship service at the end of which one of the leaders of the event pointed out the bronze plaque on the West Door.

He read it aloud: "The West Door of Cane Ridge Meeting House is dedicated to Missionaries who have responded to the call to proclaim the Word of God to all people everywhere."

He continued, "That's you. As you leave the Meeting House to commence your ministry, I encourage you to pause, say a prayer, touch the plaque, and head on to your calling."

Those words have stuck in my mind across the years as a litany of commissioning.

Sunday school teachers, before you go into those classrooms, touch the plaque. Choir, as you leave the rehearsal room and process to the sanctuary, touch the plaque. Elders, before you come to the Lord's table to offer your prayers, touch the plaque. Deacons, before you pass the trays of bread and cup to serve us, touch the plaque. Volunteers in service, before you cross the threshold of the food bank, childcare center, assisted living center, Habitat for Humanity house, prison ministry, touch the plaque. Everyone, before entering a room for a meeting, please put what you're doing in proper perspective and prepare your mind, heart, and tongue for what is to come by reaching out and touching the plaque dedicated to missionaries like you who have responded to the call to discipleship.

On my first day off after beginning my ministry in Lexington in 2014, I knew what I had to do. Jennie and I packed a picnic lunch and drove east through Paris to Cane Ridge. We ate our lunch, reminisced about visits past, then went into the Meeting House. She played the pump organ. I sat in the front row and took it all in. On the way out the West up inside yourself not giving a damn about other human be-ings! Do you hear me, David Shirey?"

Yep. That angry young man was me. And that was my dad speaking in a tongue of fire. Vavoom!

If you would have told my dad and I that a decade after that father and son tête-à-tête I'd begin a forty-year career requiring effective communication to all kinds of people in all kinds of circumstances through speaking, writing, pray-ing, and preaching, we would have dismissed it as a bunch of hooey.

Wanda picked up where my dad left off. He and she con-spired a decade apart to get through to me for my own good and the good of others. In my mind's eye, I see myself sitting across from them, arms crossed, noncommittal, face fixed, not wanting to hear what I am hearing. But my stubborn-ness is pierced by the truth of their words. An intervention is being administered, an attitude adjustment initiated from on high. The necessary words spoken, the providential chas-tening complete, I see my interrogators – Wanda and my dad. Radiating from each of them is an unmistakable aura. Vavoom!

Bad Sausage

Wanda's husband, Clarence, was on the search committee that called me to Compton Heights and Moderator
of the congregation. Midway through my third year, I asked,
"Where's Clarence? I haven't seen Clarence for several weeks.
It's not like Clarence not to be here."

I reached him by telephone and told him I missed him at
church. Was everything okay? He invited me to come to his
house. I went.

There was no small talk. Clarence launched right in and
presented a laundry list of grievances that stretched from the
Mississippi River to West County. The actions and inactions
of his church and its members had failed him.

"I want something I can die for," he said, "and right now
I wouldn't walk across the street for this church. All my sixty
years I've done what I've been told I need to do. I'm still here
and there's something in there at the center that I want and
need but I don't know how to get it."

Hard words to hear. I have no memory of how I responded, only of what he said. I wrote them verbatim in my journal.

A wise elder in the Lexington, KY, church I served from

Door, I reached out and touched the plaque. We then drove to the Seventh Street Church in Paris and remembered the day we were welcomed by Elder Reed.

Jennie and I followed God's call by being missionaries willing to be sent to nine congregations in seven states. Darrell, Marty, Kathy, Madeline, Marsha, Millie, Walt, and other Compton Heights members from my era forty years ago to today faithfully followed God's call by staying put in the pews and pavement of south St. Louis. Nearly forty years ago, we touched the plaque together. Forty years later, we are still together in service to the One who called us.

If You Ever Get to Mayfield

Marjorie was buried 200 miles southeast of St. Louis and 300 miles west of Cane Ridge in Mayfield, KY. I made the drive from St. Louis to officiate at a graveside service during which she was laid to rest in a plot next to her parents in a small cemetery down the block from a convenience store. There may have been ten people at the graveside that day in May, mostly Mayfield natives who had known Marjorie "way back when," had read of her death in the local paper, and came out to pay their respects. There were also two gravediggers who stood behind a tree, leaning on their shovels, waiting for the words to be spoken so they could finish their job, and a funeral director who reminded me several times on the way to the cemetery that he "had another one he had to get back for" and how long did I think I'd be with Miss Ford, etc. There was also Marjorie's nephew from Imperial, MO, and his wife, the only relatives Marjorie was known to have. And me.

I had been asked if there was any way I could drive down and "do a little service" when it was learned that the local Disciples preacher was out-of-town. Ten locals, two gravediggers and their shovels, one antsy funeral director, nephew Bill and his wife, and me – a congregation of sixteen at the graveside of Miss Marjorie Ford.

Suffice it to say that by the time I pronounced the benediction, those gravediggers had changed positions on their shovels numerous times and the antsy funeral director was nearly fit to be tied. I knew he "had another one he had to get back for," but I figured I had a right important one I had come down for and I didn't make a 200-mile drive just to read the 23rd Psalm, say a canned prayer, and run back to the car. So, I took my time, read all the Scriptures, prayed the prayers, and, as the funeral director impatiently shuffled his feet, delivered a brief homily which I'm certain was not as brief as he had hoped for.

At my "Amen," he stepped up and in rapid-fire fashion said, "The-service-is-now-complete-We-thank-you-for-coming-out-to-express-your-regards-for-Miss-Ford-Please-return-to-your-cars-now-We-thank-you-once-more-for-your-attendance-this-afternoon." We scurried back to our cars. As I pulled out, I saw in my rear view mirror the two gravediggers trudging toward the tent. My homily wasn't as brief as they had hoped for, either.

On the drive home, I got to feeling sort of sorry for Marjorie. She had lived seventy-eight years only to have reached the end without anyone. No family. No visiting hours. No formal funeral service. Laid to rest in rather cursory fashion in a plot next to her parents in a graveyard down the street from a convenience store. Poor Marjorie, I thought. The lady had no one.

Several months later, I received a letter from Marjorie's

nephew. Bill had been appointed executor of Marjorie's estate. After the graveside service, as we hastened back to our cars, he informed me that Marjorie had named Compton Heights Christian Church a beneficiary of her estate. I had forgotten about it until his letter arrived bearing a check in the amount of $63,200. That was $63,200 in 1987 money. That's $175,442 in 2024.

On the way back from Marjorie's graveside service, I had mourned the fact that she had no one. I take that back. I was wrong. What Marjorie had was the church. She worked for the church's National Benevolent Association, the health and social service ministries arm of our denomination. In her spare time, she participated in Compton Heights' fellowship groups such as Career Women and Christian Women's Fellowship. On Sundays, she was as regular as anyone in studying the church's book and worshipping the church's God and Christ alongside the church's people. How wrong I was in thinking that Marjorie had no one. She had the church.

I wrote to the folks at Compton Heights that we were all Marjorie had. In fitting fashion, she bequeathed to us all she had. May we be good stewards of Marjorie's money and her memory.

So, should you ever pass through Mayfield, know that there is buried there a woman of exceeding grace and generosity. Like the widow who quietly dropped two copper coins in the temple treasury, she literally gave "all she had."

Compton Heights' inheritance was a check; hers is the Lord.

Vavoom

In 1969, Compton Heights and its Five Church Association sister congregations saw a need for income-based childcare in the Shaw neighborhood. "Let the children come unto me," said Jesus. So, in order to meet the need for affordable, quality childcare, the FCA congregations founded Helping Hands Day Care Center.

When I arrived in 1985, Helping Hands was a thriving United Way of St. Louis partner agency. It was the first early childhood center in the city to receive accreditation. Housed in the education wing of Compton Heights, the presence of dozens of preschool children and their teachers along with the FCA's food bank, clothing closet, and counseling services made the three-story education building a bustling hub of community ministry. When our son Will was a toddler, we enrolled him at Helping Hands and Jennie became an assistant teacher alongside Miss Fannie who doubled on Sundays as Compton's Nursery Assistant.

I was introduced to Wanda Diedriech, Executive Director of Helping Hands and a Compton Heights member, the same afternoon I was introduced to Millie on my first visit to

St. Louis for my initial interview. Just as I was to understand my ministry to Compton Heights came with the expectation of doing ministry alongside the Five Church Association, I was likewise expected to invest time and attention in the childcare center.

Jennie volunteered the most time to Helping Hands, including putting in numerous hours at Helping Hands' most lucrative fundraiser – bingo. Held at a local V.F.W. hall, she reported many a weekday evening for bingo duty, returning home hours later shaking her head at the seriousness with which bingo devotees ply their trade and reeking of smoke and perspiration. She described how the players would take a favorite seat and then copiously set up their area with their bingo cards arranged just so, their arsenal of multicolored markers arranged just right, and trinkets strategically placed to conjure up good luck.

Her least favorite role was selling 50/50 raffle tickets, a transaction that involved spotting the raised hand of players intently marking up to a dozen cards at a time with a marker in one hand while signaling for a raffle ticket with the other. To save the distraction of reaching down to get money from their purses, the women would remove bills tucked into their bras, smush the sweaty greenbacks into Jennie's hand, then open their palm for the raffle tickets and change without missing a beat (or letter and number, as the case may be).

Fifty years later, Helping Hands, now Cornerstone Center for Early Learning, has its own building in the heart of the Shaw Neighborhood three blocks from where it was founded a half century ago under the leadership of Wanda, her husband Clarence, and other Compton Heights and Five Church

Association folks. There is no mention of bingo on their website.

One day when I stopped in Wanda's office midweek to say hello, she asked if I was aware of my aura in the pulpit.

"My aura?" I asked.

She explained that when I preach and reach inflection points in my sermon, a visible glow radiates from my head. I did my best to maintain a straight face while she illustrated my homiletical halo. Opening her hands, fingers extended, she held her palms an inch away from each ear in earmuff fashion. She then slowly moved her hands away from her head a foot or so and returned them quickly to their original position. She repeated the accordion motion several times, intoning "Vavoom!" as she did.

"Really?" I asked, feigning sincere interest to mask the incredulous guffaw that was clamoring to bust loose.

"Yes," she said, "it happens regularly," and repeated the pantomime aura accompanied by another energetic "Vavoom!"

I innocently asked Jennie at dinner that night if she noticed my aura in the pulpit and added my imitation of the expanding and contracting hands and an exclamatory "Vavoom!" When I added that a woman in the congregation had complimented me on it, she looked at me over her glasses. I quickly broke character and explained it was sixty-year-old Wanda making the observation, whereupon she suggested the aura was likely a sheen caused by excessive hairspray, not the inspiration of the Holy Spirit. I did not disagree.

Vavoom! notwithstanding, Wanda gifted me in those formative years of my ministry with a life lesson I took to heart.

"David," she said one day, "when I see you walking through the building during the week, you appear to be deep in thought. That's not a bad trait. It's just that some of our childcare teachers and parents see you in the halls. When you pass them deep in thought and don't look up to acknowledge them or say anything to them, they feel disregarded. Snubbed. I'm mentioning this to you because that's not how you want to come across to people."

Wanda's observation stung, but I could understand the dynamic she described, how my propensity to become lost in thought, oblivious to my surroundings, could be interpreted by others as aloof disinterest. *Don't bother me. I've got more important things to think about than you.* Ouch.

I was able to receive Wanda's observation for what it was, constructive criticism from one of my church's elders to a young pastor still in formation. I thanked her for pointing out how I was being perceived (Putting off a negative aura!). I promised her I would make a conscious effort when I left my office and walked the hallways to be intentional about making eye contact and warmly greeting everyone with whom I crossed paths. People seated in the waiting area of the food pantry. Parents arriving to pick up their children. Teachers shepherding their flock to the lunchroom or playground. Donald tooling up to the front door for his weekly visit. Cliff, toolbox in hand, heading to the day's fix-it project. Bob, standing in the doorway of my office unannounced with a Styrofoam cup of coffee, set to commence a fifteen-minute monologue. Darlene, our custodian, sweeping the hallway. Hazel, three-prong cane in hand, steadily shuffling to a Circle meeting in the library. Wanda's corrective in mind, I'd put on my best pastoral extroversion and engage everyone I met.

Looking back, Wanda taught me to work the room. An introvert at heart, she called forth from me the extroversion that is an absolute requirement for the relational vocation that is pastoral ministry. The demeanor I had to consciously cultivate in the hallways of Compton over time became second nature to the point that members of the congregations I've served are surprised to hear me say I'm an introvert. Wanda deserves the credit. By calling me out, she called out a more personable me.

I know a guy who when he was a teenager was an angry young man. He could cut his eyes and purse his lips just so. A master practitioner of the silent treatment, he could freeze people out. He got so mad at his parents in his early adolescence (He forgets the reason) that he determined not to speak to them. For months at a time, he refused to talk. He just nodded his head or pointed. It broke his mother's heart. It drove his dad crazy. *Why won't you talk to us?*

When he did speak once, he told his parents he knew what he wanted to be when he grew up. He'd be a hermit in Oregon – Oregon being the furthest place from home he could think of and hermit being a vocation where, in his words, he "wouldn't have to deal with people or talk to anybody. He could just be left alone." Quite a vocational aspiration, huh? Sweet kid, huh?

He says one day his father sat down across from him during one of his icy silent spells and said, "You can choose not to speak to your mother or me for the rest of our lives if you want to, but sooner or later you're going to have to learn to talk to people and relate to them. You can't live life holed

2014-2022 had held nearly every position a lay member could. He'd seen it all – the church and its people in all their glory and gory from the inside out. One day, musing over an incident when something went sideways at meeting and someone threw up their hands in exasperation, Josh folded his hands, placed them on his chest, calmly shook his head, and opined, "If you work where the sausage is made, sometimes it can make you sick to your stomach."

Clarence had a belly full of bad church bratwurst, and I had a front row seat to his spewing out his displeasure uncensored.

Milton was Clarence's soulmate in disillusionment. A retired pastor and member of the church I served in North Carolina, he was socially conscious, justice minded, intellectually astute, pastorally sensitive, and theologically grounded. However, in the years following his retirement, he lost his wife to a brain tumor, lost his confidence in the capacity of human beings to effect significant social change, and then lost his faith to boot.

I used to pick him up from his apartment and take him to Hardee's on Friday morning for a biscuit and cup of coffee. He'd unwrap his biscuit, break it open, and scrape all the bread out with a coffee stirrer, leaving only the golden-brown crust.

"David," he said one day over the hollowed-out communion of coffee and crust, "I don't believe any more. The good die young. The wicked prosper. No good deed goes unpunished. With every cause I give myself to, it's two steps forward and three steps back."

He was done with the church in all its clunkiness and

clumsiness. Done with its people in all their hypocrisy and pettiness. Done with aspiring and striving for the best only to fail, fall short, or be turned back by the worst. The good, right, and true were going down to defeat, he'd spent his life playing for a losing team, and he saw no help or hope in sight. *Stick a fork in me. I'm done!* Bad sausage.

As with Clarence's words a decade earlier, Milton's disillusionment was hard to hear. Again, I have no memory of how I responded, only of what I heard.

Clarence and Milton were not alone, of course, in walking away from the church exasperated with the enterprise, shaking their fists at God, a belly full of bile. The nineteenth-century English Romantic poet, Robert Southey, once scoffed, "I could believe in Christ if he did not drag behind him his leprous bride, the church." Some romantic, huh? An old saying goes: "To live in love with the saints above that will be glory. To live below with the saints you know is another story!" Some people – and some of God's people – are a piece of work!

Elijah scored quite a victory for God's cause on Mt. Carmel one day, but next thing you know, the tide turned as did the fickle faithful and 'ol Jezebel was after him. Whereupon the prophet hightailed it to the desert, plopped himself down under a broom tree, put his face in his hands and said, "I quit. I'm turning in my prophet card. I wouldn't walk across the street for these people!" (1 Kings 19:1-4).

A story is attributed to the late Rev. Forrest Church. When he travelled on an airplane, he used to cringe when the person seated next to him asked, "What do you do?" because when we pastors tell strangers we're ministers, we get all kinds of responses. One is to tell us they don't believe in God, to which wise Forrest Church once responded, "Tell me about the God you don't believe in. I probably don't believe in that God either."

Well played! There are indeed beliefs about God that are illusions that ought not be believed. Sometimes disillusionment is a good thing. Look at the word. Dis-illusion: to have an illusion dis-missed. Part of growing up – maturing – is to shed whatever illusions we may have, painful as that may be, so that our lives, relationships, and beliefs may be rooted in the truth.

Illusions about God include perceiving God as a Santa who gives presents to all the good girls and boys. Or God as the Lone Ranger who gallops in at the nick of time to save the innocent and punish the guilty. Or God as a genie who, when you rub the lamp, you get three prayers answered. I could go on. To believe any of them is to set oneself up for disappointment. They're illusions. Look for another God.

Likewise, there are illusions about the church and its members. Believe them and you're in for a sour stomach. It's an illusion to think the church is a place where the fruits of the Spirit –love, joy, peace, patience, kindness, gentleness, faithfulness, self-control – are in full bloom in everybody all the time in all-encompassing abundance. Neither is the church a place where "never is heard a discouraging word and the skies are not cloudy all day." Illusion!

Any relationship, if it is to last, requires disillusionment: being divested of beliefs that are not true. I thought I was marrying a woman who was an athlete, lover of classic rock music, and connoisseur of roller coasters. Not! Not! and Not!

All illusions. Should I have looked for another? Are you kidding? Do you think I'm everything Jennie thought I was? Rather than building a relationship, church membership, or faith on an illusion, it's best to be disillusioned and rebuild from a foundation of what is true.

The truth, if I might overly simplify things, is that the church is exasperating because it is comprised of human beings who are exasperating. Always have been. Always will be. Comedian A. Whitney Brown, a *Saturday Night Live* alum, quipped,

> *There's a lot we should be able to learn from history. And yet history proves that we never do. In fact, the main lesson of history is that we never learn the lessons of history. This makes us look so stupid that few people care to read it. They'd rather not be reminded. Any good history book is mainly just a long list of mistakes, complete with names and dates. It's very embarrassing.*

He could have said the same thing about the Bible. It, too, chronicles a long list of mistakes, complete with names and dates. It's very embarrassing to have the story of God's people's failed attempts at sausage making across the ages chronicled with such exasperating honesty. Things turned sideways in the Garden of Eden and have persisted ever since. We human beings become exasperated at the whole faith enterprise and walk away from it, vowing to never cross the street again to return (the largest, fastest growing denomination these days is Nones – No religious affiliation. *Done with it!*).

The gospel truth is that despite humanity's exasperating history and our propensity to exasperate, disillusion, and walk away from each other, never to cross the street again, God does not give up on us. When we walk off in a huff, God leaves a light on and the front door unlocked.

I remember as a kid throwing a temper tantrum and telling my mother I was leaving. I stomped across the kitchen where she was and let the screen door slam on the way out. Mom, unperturbed, said out the window, "If you're going to be gone forever you might get hungry. I'm getting ready to pull some chocolate chip cookies out of the oven. Maybe you want a couple of cookies and a glass of milk before you go?" I took her up on her offer and ran away as far as the back of the garage where I sat down and enjoyed my snack.

I'm talking about grace here. Grace is Elijah in the desert shaking his fist at God, "I quit! This prophet stuff is for the birds. Find somebody else." What did God do? God sent an angel with a fresh-baked cake and a jar of water. Elijah ran away from God and God sent room service (1 Kings 18:1-19:21).

Grace is Jesus. Despite his disciples – the church – having forsaken, denied, and betrayed him, he didn't walk away from them never to return. Out the Via Dolorosa he walked with the cross of our rejection on his back, crossing one street after another until he reached Golgotha. He was crucified, died, and was buried. But on the third day, having been raised from the dead, he crossed streets from Jerusalem to Galilee, appearing to his disciples along the way with the promise of his eternal, steadfast presence.

When Milton died, I led his funeral service with another pastor in our community and one of our church's elders, both of whom were aware of his flagging faith. Fred Craddock, one of the finest preachers of his era, said we all have moments when we struggle to believe. In those moments, he said, we need others to believe for us. So, Ron, Mike, and I proclaimed the resurrection, God's victory over sin and death, despair, exasperation, and disillusionment. We commended Milton into the everlasting arms in the sure and certain hope of resurrection to eternal life. Though for a season of his life Milton could not believe in God, God never ceased to believe in Milton.

I lost track of Clarence and Wanda after I left Compton Heights in 1989. Thirty-five years later, I was doing an interim ministry in Columbia, MO. I was remembering him and Wanda and composing these chapters in their memory. I googled their names and found obituaries. Wanda died at age seventy in 1997. Clarence lived to the age of ninety-six, dying in 2022. They were members of Lake Ozark Christian Church (Disciples of Christ) in Missouri. A pastor I knew years ago did Wanda's funeral. One of his successors officiated at Clarence's. Maybe Clarence's faith in God, humanity, and the church had been restored. Chastened. Deepened.

The obituary read:

Clarence served in the United States Army during World War II receiving a Purple Heart. He was a member of the Lake Ozark Christian Church of Lake Ozark, MO, and was employed as an accountant for Union Electric for many years. He was one of the founders of Cornerstone Center for Early Learning in St. Louis, MO. He was a proud supporter of multiple children's organizations and Native American orga-

nizations. Clarence was a wonderful husband, father and grandfather.

The obituaries named the cemetery Clarence and Wanda are buried in. It is an hour's drive south of Columbia. I knew what I needed to do. When Clarence told me in his living room, "Right now I wouldn't walk across the street for this church," I had no response. Thirty-five years later, I did. I'd walk across the street and then some for him on behalf of the church, its members, and its risen Lord. I'd make a trip from where I sat in Columbia to where they were buried an hour south.

I did. I drove an hour, found the rural cemetery, parked the car, and wandered through the gravestones until I saw their names. I knelt and touched the stone in respectful silence to honor the memory of two people who had been formative in my life, servants of their nation, their church, and a half century's worth of children.

On the way back, I pulled into an old-timey roadside drive-in in Eldon, MO, that boasted footlong chili dogs. I ordered one with the works – chili, cheese, onions, mustard. It was the closest thing to sausage I could find.

It was delicious.

Letter of Thanksgiving

I retired from forty years of congregational ministry on August 21, 2022. Three months later, November of 2022, Jennie and I drove to St. Louis for a surprise birthday weekend with our youngest daughter. Laura, her husband Ryan, Jennie and I attended worship at Compton Heights on Sunday morning. It had been thirty-seven years since I flew into St. Louis Lambert International airport and was chauffeured by Fred Kaley. My heart was full to be back. I saw a few familiar faces, still faithful after all these years, among them Darrell and Marty Hughes. Jennie and I have maintained a friendship with Darrell and Marty over the four decades since our ministry alongside them in St. Louis. Darrell's parents, Cliff and Edna, are gone, but their love for the church and selfless service to neighbors near and far is continued in Darrell and Marty's steadfast devotion to Compton Heights and its ministries. There are none finer. We went out for lunch after worship and reminisced, naming many of the names whose stories I've shared in these pages. Jennie and I left that meal with cups overflowing – our bodies, minds, hearts, and spirits full.

Below is the letter I sent to Darrell and Marty after our visit.

***

November 22, 2022

Dear Darrell and Marty,

It was so good to be back at Compton Heights on Sunday morning for worship. It did my heart good to be at the place that blessed Jennie and me on our way through forty years of ministry.

As I may have mentioned to you, I've worked for fifteen years with young pastors as a mentor for a ministry called Bethany Fellows. I've come to believe that the first full-time congregation a pastor serves molds his/her disposition toward ministry for the rest of his/her life. If it is a good situation – healthy church, people supportive of their pastor, a congregation committed to caring for one another and serving those beyond their doorsteps – pastors will have a positive view of congregational ministry. If, on the other hand, the first experience is marked by dysfunction and conflict, criticism and cliquishness, the absence of a wide-armed welcome and sacrificial service, pastors develop a negative attitude and either leave congregational ministry altogether at the ripe old age of twenty-seven or they approach all future calls with suspicion and apprehension.

My years at Compton made me love what I was blessed to be able to do for four decades in nine churches in seven states – be a congregational pastor.

Seeing you two, Millie, Marsha, Madeline, Judi, Kathy, and dear Walt reminded me of dozens of others who worshipped, learned, and served from 2149 S. Grand in years gone by. As we worshipped on Sunday, one of the verses in the choir's anthem began with the words "Thank you for the elders...." I could see those blessed elders in my mind's eye in their regular spots. We named many of their names on Sunday over lunch. I remember many occasions subsequent to my years at Compton when I included them in sermons and newsletter articles. I've printed out a few of those and have included them for your enjoyment. Blessed be the tie that binds!

There is a DNA at Compton Heights that endures throughout the decades, undiminished through the years. CHCC is a church that serves all God's children in a scope and manner that far exceeds its size and resources. There are untold numbers of churches twice to ten times the size of Compton whose footprint of service and witness in Christ's name is a fraction of what is done from S. Grand and Flora Place.

Evidence of that enduring Compton spirit was seeing and hearing you two in the choir, Darrell as liturgist, watching Kathy care for her uncle Walt and lovingly lead Lucy out of the sanctuary for whatever is done now with Children's Church (Carol Mead all over again), hearing that Madeline has accepted the Moderator's position with the Mid-America Region, and Marsha and Judi's participation during the Offering and at the Lord's Table. Disciples of Christ, indeed!

My Thanksgiving Week is marked by gratitude for our lifelong friendship.

Grace and peace to you two until we're together again.

In Christ,

David

Epilogue: Jeremiah's Memo

We ... must determine what our role should be in the community. This immediately raises the principal problem of the city and the city church: the move of the people to the suburbs. Should churches follow their membership? If so, what will happen to the center of the city, which is considered by many to be a very important factor in our national culture? ... Our membership is spread over the Metropolitan area. This is a problem, but it is also an opportunity. Here is a place where people from suburbs and apartments, from all social and economic levels, from all age groups come together. We can be a living demonstration that Christian love can bind people of different backgrounds and interests together ... This is the area where we are called to witness and save. This is part of our mission.

–The Rev. Dr. G. Hugh Wilson, 1961

"Seek the welfare of the city where I have sent you ... and pray to the Lord on its behalf, for in its welfare you will find your welfare"

–Jeremiah 29:7

I dub Jeremiah the patron saint of urban ministry, progenitor of all saints of the city. I'll come back to him in a moment, but first, let's take a brief windshield tour of the Bible to see how the city is viewed in Scripture. Don't worry, we won't be stopping at any Public Works projects, just Scriptures germane to urban ministry.

The Bible begins in a garden. Out in the country, if you will. Are we closer to God in the country – in nature – than in the city? Psalm 23 says, "The Lord is my shepherd, I shall not want." That's rural imagery. It's not "The Lord is my mayor, I shall not lack any municipal services." Psalm 121 is "I lift up my eyes to the hills," not "I lift up my eyes to the Gateway Arch."

At first blush, cities get a bad rap in the Bible. The first city is founded by Cain (Genesis 4:17) – a murderer. The next urban development is the Tower of Babel. Then Sodom. Then come the prophets who point their fingers at the manifold sins of cities. Jerusalem is indicted for all sorts of injustice and immorality. Nineveh, capital of Assyria, and Babylon, capital of Babylonia, are skewered for idolatry. When Jesus surveys Jerusalem from the Mount of Olives, what does he do? Does he take a smiling selfie against the Jerusalem skyline? No. He weeps, saying, "If you only knew the things that make for peace" (Luke 19:32). How was Rome portrayed by John in Revelation? "The mother of harlots and of earth's abominations" (Revelation 17:5). That's not Chamber of Commerce material. The Bible has its share of anti-urban perspective.

But what do you make of this? The Bible begins in a garden but ends in a city. John sees "a new Jerusalem coming down out of heaven" (Revelation 21:2), not an unspoiled countryside. God's salvation is inclusive of single souls, but its ultimate aim is all civilization. The author of the Letter to the Hebrews looks forward to "the city which has foundations, whose builder and maker is God" (Hebrews 11:10). Talk about urban renewal!

The city as the goal of God's redeeming work is an end unique to Judaism and Christianity. The ultimate end of other religions is different. In Islam, humanity's final destiny is a garden oasis where individual needs are met. In Eastern religions, the end of humankind is mystic union with the Ultimate in which all social relations are transcended.

Jesus made his life's journey with laser-like focus toward a city. He was dragged outside its gates to be crucified (*We don't want your redemption!*), but raised up, he did not give up on the city. He promised the Holy Spirit which, on the Day of Pentecost, was poured out upon a United Nations of humanity in a building in the middle of a city (Acts 2:1-31). The church was born in a city and sent to redeem all cities.

Back to Jeremiah's Memo. Jeremiah sent word from God, saying, "Seek the welfare of the city where I have sent you in exile" (Jeremiah 29:7). Urban ministry was born. The word translated *welfare* is better translated *shalom*—a word that might be best translated *comprehensive flourishing*. Seek the comprehensive flourishing of which city? Babylon! Taken captive from beloved Jerusalem by the archenemy Babylonians, God told the people to seek the welfare of the city of Babylon. What an outrageous, outlandish … outstanding thing to say! As Andy Crouch wrote in *A New Kind of Urban Ministry*, "Even when God's people sojourn among neighbors who want nothing to do with God, they should actively seek their neighbors' flourishing." There is no us and them in God's vision for a city. *Us* and *them* are both part of God's we. God seeks the welfare of all God's children, Babylonians and Jerusalemites.

Compton Heights Christian Church (Disciples of Christ) received Jeremiah's Memo to "seek the welfare of the city where I have sent you." That word *sent* in Latin is *missio* from which we get our words *mission*. *Missio*naries are folks *sent* to certain places to seek the welfare of that place. Since its founding 130 years ago, Compton Heights has understood its mission to be a church serving the city. They've reaffirmed that throughout the years. During decades of white flight to the suburbs, many congregations founded in urban neighborhoods relocated to county pastures. Not Compton. They stayed and sought the welfare of the hurly-burly, bawdy, boisterous city.

The congregation's location is a bricks and mortar testimony to its mission to pew and pavement. The sanctuary is next to a Jack in the Box fast food restaurant. On any given Sunday when the windows are open, a worshipper can hear "This is the Word of God" intoned from the pulpit microphone while the loudspeaker across the adjoining parking lot blares, "One Jumbo Jack Combo – hold the onions – fries and a Coke. Is there anything else I can get for you?" Sacred and secular, holy and mundane, are inextricably linked on South Grand.

Jeremiah's Memo: "Seek the welfare of the city where I have sent you."

Hugh Wilson: "We can be a living demonstration that Christian love can bind people of different backgrounds and interests together ... This is the area where we are called to witness and save. This is part of our mission."

Cliff on the roof praying for urban neighbors as far as his eye could see.

Millie's arms and heart opened as wide as the skyline's horizon.

Wanda welcoming God's children of all races, ethnicities, and incomes.

Compton Heights' century-plus ministry from pew to pavement, from worship of God to service of all God's children.

Memo received.

***

After four years alongside the saints of Compton Heights, I was called to First Christian Church (Disciples of Christ), Wilmington, NC. Another stretch, another story.

I look back on the four formative years of my life and ministry in St. Louis and give thanks for what could have been and what was.

I could have stayed in my comfort zone and never accepted a call west of the Mississippi. I could have accepted the call of the Iowa congregation and learned to do ministry in soybean and corn fields.

I could have responded to Elder Reed's letter and explored the possibility of serving a historic African American congregation.

Instead, I got to serve as pastor of Compton Heights Christian Church.

Count me blessed.

Notes

Introduction: No April Fools

The first four quotations in the epigraph are from Agnes J. Sierat-Taylor, *A Brief History: Compton Heights Christian Church (1894-1994)*.

"I am convinced that the journey began long, long ago": The Rev. Dr. Jacque Foster, "How Did We Get Here?" 2001.

"It killed more people in less time than any other disaster in St. Louis history": St. Louis Public Library Digital Collections. Tornado of 1896 Collection. (https://cdm17210. contentdm.oclc.org/digital/collection/p17210coll3#:~:-text=Louis%20on%20May%2027%2C%201896,the%20 topic%20of%20the%20tornado.&text=It%20killed%20 more%20people%20in,Louis%20history)

"In the judgment of many, it is not worth repairing": "Celebrating our 130th Anniversary"(https://comptonheights. com/2024/07/21/130th-anniversary/)

"The Church exists by mission, just as a fire exists by burning": Emil Brunner, The Word and the World (London: World Student Movement, 1931).

Somewhere East of the Mississippi

"For nearly three years, I served the Carthage (TN) Christian Church (Disciples of Christ)": Stories from my ministry in Carthage are chronicled in my book *It Don't Get Any Better Than This: Stories from a Small-Town Church.*

"We live life forward, but understand it backward": Søren Kierkegaard, *Journals and Papers* (1843).

What the Stonemason Said

"Make a good shoe and sell it at a fair price": Some dispute these were Luther's actual words, but he did speak eloquently about vocation and the spirituality of ordinary life.

Look for a Steeple

"Home is the place where when you have to go there, they have to take you in": Robert Frost, *North of Boston* (New York: Henry Holt and Company, 1915).

A Barber's Prayers

"lest you think Cliff's steeple supplications were but a 'sweet hour of prayer'": an allusion to the hymn "Sweet Hour of Prayer." Words: William Walford. Music: William Bradbury. *Chalice Hymnal*, 1995, p. 570.

Isaiah 58 Ministries' Mission Statement is on their website. (https://i58ministries.org/about/)

First Among Equals

"John Wesley said, 'The world is my parish'": In a letter dated June 11, 1739: "I have now no parish of my own, nor probably ever shall… I look upon all the world as my parish."

Gold Stamp Guarantee

"Five months of fire, brimstone, and plagues on Earth": Kimberly Winston (March 23, 2011): "Judgement Day: May 21, 2011." *Washington Post.*

"If your church vanished, would your community weep?": Eric Swanson and Rick Rusaw, *The Externally Focused Church* (Group Publishing, 2004).

The Acorn Does Not Fall Far from the Tree

"a non-anxious presence": Edwin H. Friedman, *A Failure of Nerve: Leadership in the Age of the Quick Fix* (Seabury Books, 2007).

Every Day is Gravy

"I didn't realize. So all that was going on and we never noticed": Thornton Wilder, *Our Town* (New York: Harper & Row, 1938).

"Attention is the beginning of devotion": Mary Oliver, *Upstream: Selected Essays* (New York: Penguin Press, 2016).

"Listen to your life. See it for the fathomless mystery it is": Frederick Buechner, *Now and Then: A Memoir of Vocation* (HarperOne, 1991).

"The only commandment I ever obeyed was 'Consider the lilies.'": Emily Dickinson, Letters from Dickinson to Alice Tuckerman, June 1884.

"Do you think there is anything not attached by its unbreakable cord to everything else?": Mary Oliver, *Upstream: Selected Essays* (New York: Penguin Press, 2016).

"Our basic work in life is learning to be astonished": Mary Oliver, *Thirst* (Boston: Beacon Press, 2006).

Kneeling

"Are we going to live this life from our knees?": Eugene Peterson, *Leap Over a Wall* (HarperCollins, 1997), p. 42.

Why?

"theodicy": (https://www.britannica.com/search?query=theodicy)

"I remembered a story Leslie Weatherhead, a British pastor, told": *The Will of God*, Leslie Weatherhead (Nashville: Abingdon Press, 1982), pp. 10-11, 14-15.

"The implication is everything happens the way it does because it's God's will for it to happen that way": Adam Hamilton explores this phrase and its implications in a chapter entitled "Where Is God When Bad Things Happen?" in his book *Seeing Gray in a World of Black and White*

(Nashville: Abingdon Press, 2008, pp. 121-132).

"The resurrection means the worst thing is never the last thing": Frederick Buechner, *The Final Beast* (New York: Atheneum, 1965).

"The late William Sloane Coffin lost a son decades ago": Read Dr. Coffin's eulogy for his son at (http://www. pbs. org/now/printable/transcript_eulogy_print. html)

Orientation: Joyful

"Joy happens when God is present and people know it": Barbara Brown Taylor, "Surprised by Joy," *The Living Pulpit* (Oct-Dec 1996):16.

"Spirituals took away their shame, wiped away their tears and made them part of God's own family": Marjory Zoet Bankson, "With Shouts of Joy," *The Living Pulpit* (Oct-Dec 1996):9.

"I learned the etymology – the origin – of the word content": (https://www.etymonline.com/word/content)

A Woman's Testimony

"From women let not evidence be accepted because of the levity and temerity of their sex": cf. Yeb. 88b, 115a; Mishnah, Rosh Hashana 1. 8. quoted in *The New Testament Concept of Witness*, Alison Trites, p. 54.

The Laughing Man

"When In Our Music God is Glorified," Words: Fred Pratt Green. Music: Charles Stanford. *Chalice Hymnal*, 1995, p. 7.

"Listen to your life": Frederick Buechner, *Now and Then: A Memoir of Vocation* (HarperOne, 1991).

"a room he dubbed the Magic Kingdom.": Frederick Buechner, *The Eyes of the Heart: A Memoir of the Lost and Found* (HarperCollins, 1999), p. 1.

Roach Wrath

"The day the squirrel went berserk": "Mississippi Squirrel Revival," Ray Stevens. From his 1984 album *He Thinks He's Ray Stevens*.

Wrestling with God

"Max Lucado describes such moments as 'anvil time.': Max Lucado, *On the Anvil: Stories of Being Shaped into God's Image* (Wheaton, Ill.: Tyndale House, 1985).

Tribute

"an entry in the database of Notable Kentucky African Americans": (https://nkaa.uky.edu/nkaa/items/show/435)

Bad Sausage

"I could believe in Christ if he did not drag behind him his leprous bride": quoted in William Willimon, *What's Right with the Church* (HarperCollins Publishers, 1985).

Epilogue: Jeremiah's Memo

"We ... must determine what our role should be in the community": The Rev. Dr. G. Hugh Wilson quoted in Agnes J. Sierat-Taylor, *A Brief History: Compton Heights Christian Church (1894-1994)*.

"Even when God's people sojourn among neighbors who want nothing to do with God, they should actively seek their neighbors' flourishing": Andy Crouch, "A New Kind of Urban Ministry," *Christianity Today*, November 2011.

www.ingramcontent.com/pod-product-compliance
Lightning Source LLC
Chambersburg PA
CBHW020858090426
42736CB00008B/425